(2)

THE BORING DAYS AND AWESOME NIGHTS OF ROY WINKLESTEEN

By
Sally Dill

Thinkbutton, Inc.
Charlotte, North Carolina

Copyright © 2020 Sally Dill
No part of this book may be reproduced or used in any manner without the express written permission of the publisher except for the use of brief quotations in a book review.

This is a work of fiction. Names, characters, businesses, places, events and incidents are either the products of the author's imagination or used in a fictitious manner. Any resemblance to actual persons, living or dead, or actual events is purely coincidental.

Thinkbutton, Inc.
Charlotte, North Carolina
thinkbutton.com

Visit the author's website at:
sallydill.com

ISBN: 978-0-9996671-2-5

*To all the people of the world
who don't need a place in the sun
because they shine from within.*

ACKNOWLEDGMENTS

Thank you for your guidance.

Debby Tamura MS, RN, APNG
Laboratory of Cancer Biology and Genetics
Center for Cancer Research
National Cancer Institute
https://clinicaltrials.gov/
https://ccr.cancer.gov/laboratory-of-cancer-biology-and-genetics

Jonah Gollub, PhD
Center for Metamaterials and Integrated Plasmonics
Duke University
http://metamaterials.duke.edu/

TitaniumAmy and Janice Hansen, PhD
https://titaniumamyblog.wordpress.com/

CONTENTS

CHAPTER 1
Strange. *1*

CHAPTER 2
Ugh . . . *6*

CHAPTER 3
Busted! *12*

CHAPTER 4
Whatever. *23*

CHAPTER 5
Huh? *37*

CHAPTER 6
Seriously! *51*

CHAPTER 7
Whew. *62*

CHAPTER 8
Promise? *68*

CONTENTS

CHAPTER 9
Trust Me. *76*

CHAPTER 10
No Way! *82*

CHAPTER 11
Awesome! *94*

CHAPTER 12
Oops. *107*

CHAPTER 13
Ha . . . Ha, Very Funny. *119*

CHAPTER 14
Guess Who? *130*

CHAPTER 15
Ffffrrrrrrrrrrt. *137*

CHAPTER 16
Don't Worry. *146*

CHAPTER 17
Be Cool. *160*

CHAPTER 18
Like magic. *169*

CHAPTER 19
Really? *178*

CHAPTER 20
Ahh . . . *185*

CHAPTER 21
Loser. *196*

CHAPTER 22
Finally. *202*

CHAPTER 23
Enough Already. *211*

CHAPTER 24
Boo! *220*

CHAPTER 25
Ouch! *232*

CHAPTER 26
Bravo. *245*

2
THE BORING DAYS AND AWESOME NIGHTS OF ROY WINKLESTEEN

CHAPTER 1

STRANGE.

Roy stared out his bedroom window.

It was nine o'clock on a Saturday morning. Typically, he would be sleeping in.

But not today.

Roy's neighborhood actually had something interesting going on, and the clouds moved out of the way so that the sun's rays could spotlight all the activity. Along with the glaring light beaming past his half-closed curtains, the muffled voices and clamoring from outside had beckoned Roy awake. His curiosity had gotten the best of him, and before he knew it, he had been looking out his window for over an hour.

A new family was moving in across the street two houses to the left in the one-story home that had been vacant for almost a year.

Roy laughed as two overstuffed moving men tried to cram an overstuffed couch through the home's too-skinny doorway. It didn't seem to matter which way they turned the piece of furniture. It didn't fit horizontally or vertically or at any angle in between. The couch was about two inches fatter than the doorway was wide.

Roy leaned closer to his window as the two flustered movers plunked the hefty piece of furniture down on the front porch and looked at each other like the problem was unsolvable. Then another man, about half the size of one of the movers, appeared in the doorway from inside the house. He peered above the petite, black-framed glasses barely clinging to the end of his nose and pondered over the problem for a few seconds. After a brief but rather lively discussion, all three men hammered out the bolts from the hinges and removed the burgundy-colored front door.

The movers lifted the couch, angled it slightly, and slid it through the opening like it had been slathered with butter. Roy continued to watch in wonder as the men paraded back and forth through the doorless opening, lugging pieces of furniture that represented about every decade from the past 100 years. After they had conquered all the big stuff, they continued by hauling in boxes of all sizes and wooden crates with the word "fragile" faintly painted in red.

Obviously, everything going into the house had originated from much more interesting places than Roy's boring little city. In fact, they were shoving so much stuff into the smallest house on the street that Roy expected the structure to start bulging out like his suitcase had when he'd packed for his out-of-town math competition.

"Whatcha lookin' at, nosey?" Roy spun around to find Melonie behind him.

"What do you think I'm looking at?" he said to his little sister. "I'm looking at the same thing all the other neighbors are looking at."

"Do you think they have any kids?" Melonie climbed up on Roy's desk to get a closer look.

"I dunno. All I've seen is a man and two movers."

"I hope they have a girl my age, and I hope she likes dolls and makeup and—"

"Yeah . . . and maybe her name will be Melonie too." Roy rolled his eyes.

"Stop being such a smart-butt." Melonie hopped off his desk. "Mom wants you downstairs . . . now."

"Tell her I'll be there in a minute."

"Better hurry."

Roy blew off his little sister's threat and fixated on a black car that pulled up behind the moving van. A woman got out and walked around to the other side of the car. She opened the door, and a kid wearing a white, large-brimmed hat got out. As they walked toward the house, Roy narrowed in on the kid. The hat hid a lot, but the long hair flowing down to the waist and the pink pants made it pretty clear he was looking at a girl.

As she turned toward the woman, Roy got a glimpse of something strange. The hat the girl was wearing was not an ordinary hat. It looked a little like something he had seen a beekeeper wearing on TV. He also noticed large, dark sunglasses that seemed to swallow her face. She was also wearing gloves.

Gloves? Roy thought. He opened his window and stuck his hand out. It felt like a jeans and short-sleeve day. Maybe long sleeves like the girl was wearing—but gloves—it was definitely too warm to even think about gloves. And that weird hat? Was she in some type of costume or disguise? Why? Was she famous? Was she hiding from someone? Did she see someone get murdered and was now part of a witness protection program?

Roy retrieved his binoculars from his desk drawer.

He attempted to get a closer look, but both figures disappeared into the house. The man with the dark-framed glasses walked out with the movers and stood in the driveway until the van drove out of sight. He returned to the house, where he struggled to hang the front door back on the hinges.

In a matter of minutes, the house looked almost as uninteresting as it had before the people moved in.

As Roy removed the binoculars from his face, his forehead furrowed with confusion. Just as his mind began to churn with ideas, things across the street got even weirder.

Right as Roy looked back at the house, he noticed that all the curtains—which had been opened for almost a year—were being yanked shut so that no gap was visible between them.

Why would they close the curtains during the day? Roy wondered. Weren't curtains typically opened to let sunlight in?

He studied the house. It somehow looked sadder and more off-limits than it had when no one was living in it.

Roy wasn't sure what to think. But he did know what to do.

It was time to gather up all of his spy gear for a closer look.

CHAPTER 2

UGH...

Roy sat halfway on his desk so that he could achieve the optimum position for watching the home. With his binoculars firmly against his face, he scanned the shady yard for signs of any other bizarre behavior or people. For most families, moving day typically required a lot of movement, which should have given Roy lots to spy on. But even if there wasn't, he happily welcomed the distraction—no matter how mundane.

His brain needed something else to think about other than middle school.

His arms started to cramp, so he decided to rely on his eleven-year-old vision to alert him of any suspicious activity. As the view outside his window became less promising by the minute, Roy's mind shifted from spy-mode to red-alert worry.

Middle School: For the first two months, sixth grade hadn't been nearly as scary as Roy had anticipated. Sure, the building was bigger, and so were the kids. Still, he was adjusting comfortably by tapping into some of the confidence he had acquired over the summer.

He was quite proud of himself.

That is, until about three days ago when a huge problem forced its way into Roy's life. It was so big that it had become an oozing scab leaking into every compartment of his brain and infecting almost everything that made him happy. As a matter of fact, it was making him misera—

"Roy, didn't you hear me?" He slid around so fast that he kicked his desk lamp onto the floor. "If you are going to sit on your desk, please be careful." His mom pursed her freshly glossed lips. Roy placed the lamp back on the desk. "Get your shoes on. We're going shopping."

Roy returned his binoculars to the drawer and let out a series of exaggerated sighs as he fumbled around his room in search of his shoes. "Why can't you and Melonie go? I hate shopping."

Roy's mom made it clear that she didn't have time for his complaining. "Because I said so. Now, hurry up.

I'll be waiting in the car."

Roy wriggled his feet into his untied sneakers and thumped down the stairs to the back door.

Normally, he wouldn't have to go shopping. Instead, he'd be helping his dad with some home improvement project. But on this particular Saturday, his dad had to work, so Roy had to hang out with the girls. Ugh. He should've stayed in bed and played the stomachache routine.

He reached his mom's already-running car just as she let out the first honk. Melonie was strapped in the backseat, showing off a missing-tooth grin. Roy locked himself in beside her and shot her an ugly look. He knew why she was happy. She knew how bad he didn't want to be there. But Roy wasn't going to give her the satisfaction of enjoying his misery, so he decided to take advantage of the situation.

"While we're out, can we stop by Sofasports?" Roy paused and locked his big, dark eyes on his sister. "I've saved some of my allowance and want to get a new game."

"That's fine," his mom said while looking in the rearview mirror. "See? I guess shopping isn't all bad."

Roy gave her a smile and then looked back at Melonie. She stuck out her tongue, crossed her arms, and looked away. Roy settled back into the seat. There was nothing better than putting your little sister in her place, he thought.

"What are we shopping for, anyway?" Roy asked.

"We need to get something for the new neighbors," his mom said. "We want to make them feel welcome, don't we?" She turned around and glanced his way.

"Uh-huh" was all he said. His mind was too busy thinking about how this shopping trip was turning out to be a great idea. Bringing the new neighbors a gift—Roy couldn't have thought of a better way to find out more about the mysterious girl in the strange outfit, the closed curtains, and the fragile items in the crates.

Certainly, a gift would get his family into the house. And the better the gift, the longer the neighbors might let them stay, giving Roy more time to spy.

Roy's body tingled with excitement. "What do you think we should get?"

"Well, food is always nice to receive when you're busy moving in. You know . . . not really time to cook," his mom said.

"I think we should get them some gummy worms," Melonie chimed in. "Everybody likes those."

Roy sneered at her. She was going to blow it. If the new neighbors found out how annoying she was, Roy would never get close to them. "Gummy worms?" Roy huffed. "No one eats gummy worms for dinner. They need real food. You know, the kind you never like to eat. Just think of the stuff you hate, and that's what we should get them."

"Gummy worms are a good idea." Melonie's blond locks bounced up and down as she snipped back at her big brother. "How does broccoli say 'welcome to the neighborhood?' It's not fun. Besides, if they have kids, they'll like them."

"All right, you two," their mom interrupted. "You both have the right idea. Maybe we can get them a basket and put practical and fun items to eat in it. That way, we can make everyone in their family feel welcome."

For the rest of the car ride, Roy and Melonie didn't bother continuing the argument. They both knew that Helen Winklesteen's vortex of logic was where opposing opinions met their demise.

At the final store of the day, they filled up the shopping cart with all sorts of goodies. There were cracker boxes with foreign writing, luscious-looking fruits, cookies that looked homemade, cheese representing almost every geometric shape Roy could think of, and, of course, gummy worms. They even picked out a wicker basket to put it all in. It was a mouth-watering sight and bound to impress (and distract) the new neighbors. Roy snickered at the idea that his mom had made his spying efforts easier.

When they returned home, his mom put everything away and began preparing dinner.

Roy couldn't contain his excitement. "What about the neighbors? Aren't we going to give them the basket?"

"Oh, it can wait until tomorrow," his mom said, not looking up from the potatoes she was cutting. "Your dad won't be home in time, and I want him to meet them too."

Roy slouched his way up the stairs and plopped his backside onto his desk chair. Tomorrow—always tomorrow or the next day. Never now. As usual, Roy would have to wait.

He leaned over his desk and looked out the window. The tiny house with the strange girl inside had not changed since he last saw it.

Roy opened his game. For now, helping Inspector Shiftybrows solve the latest murder in Dreadville would have to keep his mind busy.

CHAPTER 3

BUSTED!

After dinner, Roy watched his mom arrange all the treats in the basket. He wished he had her delicate touch and precision. She made everything look like it belonged in a display case.

"How's that?" she asked him, turning the basket toward him so that the bow on the handle faced him.

"I'd like it if I were a new neighbor." Roy's mouth was watering so much he had to swallow twice.

"Are there any gummy worms left over?" Melonie worked her way between Roy and his mom.

"No, sweetie," their mom said as she positioned the basket like a piece of art in the center of the kitchen table. "But you can each have a cookie."

Melonie shoved Roy out of the way and beat him to the pantry to grab the bag of cookies. Roy's dad,

Charles Royston Winklesteen II, came into the kitchen to get one as well. "I talked to Larry down the street, and they said they thought the new neighbors had a kid right around your age, Roy."

"Oh, that would be great." Helen Winklesteen looked at Roy like he'd won some sort of prize. "You could be their school buddy. It's always so hard going to a new school, especially after the year is already underway."

Roy snuck several cookies and headed upstairs. "Yeah, maybe," he mumbled, not sure he wanted to be a girl's "buddy."

"I guess we'll find out tomorrow," his dad said. Then he scooped up Melonie, flung her over his shoulder, and walked toward the den. "C'mon, Mel. Let's go watch some TV." His mom followed them, and Roy made his way up to his room.

It had been a typical day at the Winklesteen house, where the family, once again, devoured the same recipe for life: two parts predictability mixed with one part cautiousness sprinkled with a pinch of properness and all whipped into a perfect batter of boring.

Fortunately, nights followed days, and Roy was looking forward to any excitement the darkness might bring. He settled in at his desk and tried to finish the pile of homework his middle-school teachers felt they had to assign to distinguish themselves from the softer, more nurturing elementary school instructors.

As the sun set behind a silhouette of trees and homes, a golden glow transformed his room into a cozy hideaway. He loved being a nightlifer. Every evening, when the sky dimmed, life swept all the chaos from the sunlit hours under the bed, freeing time and space so that brilliant ideas could stretch out, take a deep breath, and re-energize.

Night was the perfect time to ponder, plan, and produce. He hadn't bothered telling anyone how he felt because he hadn't thought anyone else felt the same way—until this past summer break.

If Roy had never looked out his bedroom window at 2 a.m., he would have never discovered that he shared his passion for the night with such an elite group of people—like Bart, a genius inventor who used to live one street over. Sometimes, he couldn't believe that he had spent almost every summer night with a man that had accomplished feats engineers only dreamed of conquering.

It had been the most awesome time of Roy's life, and he had vowed to keep his nights with Bart a secret—no matter what. It was hard not to tell the whole world about all the mind-blowing inventions he had seen and used in Bart's workshop. But being a trustworthy nightlifer was how he got to spend time with Bart and how he would probably get to know other remarkable nightlifers. Why blow it? Roy asked himself.

Besides, Bart was his friend, and trust bonds friends together for life, even when you can't be around them. When Roy thought about it, he didn't find it hard to keep his friend's inventions a secret. He agreed with Bart's philosophy that daylifers weren't ready to deal with such greatness. And perhaps weren't deserving, either. They didn't understand or appreciate nightlifers and didn't accommodate them in any way. So, why should they partake in the privilege of what nightlifers were accomplishing?

Roy looked up from his essay and locked his stare on the house where Bart used to live. The attic window that had once offered a view out of Bart's workshop was totally black. The new owners had no idea what amazing accomplishments had occurred in a space they probably used for storage. But Roy knew, and he would do anything to see his friend leap off the roof and soar into the night sky just one more time.

A lump formed in Roy's throat; he attempted to blink the watery blurriness from his eyes. He missed his nighttime friend: their talks, the laughter, Bart's strange but surprisingly sensible view of the world, and all his fantastic stories of fighting crime. Bart was the smartest person he had ever known, and Roy had learned more from his genius neighbor in one summer than he had learned in an entire year of school. When he was with Bart, Roy was at his best. But now that Bart was no longer in his life, he was beginning to worry that the confident and brave boy of last summer was dwindling away and the insecure and ignored boy from elementary school was manifesting within himself a little more every day.

If only Bart hadn't moved an entire state away, Roy would have his middle-school dilemma solved by now. Nothing and no one stood in Bart's way. He could be who he wanted. He could create what he wanted (most of it out of other people's garbage), and best of all, he could solve any problem. And when Roy was around Bart, he felt like he could do anything too. That's why Roy wanted to be just like Bart when he grew up.

He wondered what Bart was doing now—in his new workshop—in his new home. Would he ever see his nightlifer friend again?

For now, the only people in his life were daylifers, all droning about, totally consumed with daylifer obligations. They were okay, Roy thought. The world certainly needed them. But he didn't always understand them. And he knew they didn't understand him. Daylifers appeared mindless in the monotony of doing the same old thing yesterday, today, and the day after. Didn't they realize the sun was laughing at them—gobbling up minutes and teasing them with the possibility of disappearing before they had completed all the stuff they didn't want to do in the first place? It all seemed kind of hopeless to Roy, and he was glad he knew better.

He shifted his eyes back to his essay. He still had quite a bit to write, and feeling sorry for himself was doing nothing but wasting time. Besides, the view outside his window had taken a slight turn toward the interesting. Roy needed to get his homework done so he could concentrate on something he knew he was good at: spying.

He shoved all his gloomy thoughts to the back of his brain. Why bother thinking about things he could do nothing about? Maybe the new view out his window presented a new adventure or, at the very least, a new friend.

Roy finished up his homework and let his extreme daylifer parents officially tuck him in. He waited a while before sneaking out of bed to begin his investigation. After confirming the rest of the Winklesteens were asleep, he aimed his binoculars at the new neighbor's house. To his surprise, the curtains that had been so attentively closed during the day were now pushed wide open. He zoomed in on the large bay window right next to the porch. He could see some boxes and shadows, but that was about it.

Roy soon lost interest in the window and panned the front of the house in search of anything that could reveal more about the strange girl.

It didn't take him long to find a clue.

It was staring right at him.

Roy jerked the binoculars away from his eyes and dove to the floor.

He froze for a moment before sitting up and fully grasping what his binoculars had revealed.

It was that girl—the one in the pink pants—standing under a tree in her front yard and looking at him with a set of binoculars even bigger than his.

But how could she see him?

Roy pivoted around and perused his room. He noticed the problem immediately. A yellowish halo surrounded his closed closet door. What a sloppy spy he was. How could he have forgotten to turn off the light?

He sat on the floor. He felt like a fool. The pink pants girl had caught him spying.

Roy rested his elbows on his knees and cupped his chin with his hands. He wasn't sure how long he should stay out of view of the window. Was she still standing there, waiting for him to emerge so she could catch him again?

Roy looked at the Ooberleeben survival watch his dad had given him. It was almost 11 p.m.

What was she doing out so late? Didn't she have a bedtime? Didn't her parents care? Wasn't she afraid to be out there all alone—so exposed—almost begging for someone to kidnap her? How could she possibly know the neighborhood was so safe and boring? Was someone from inside the house keeping an eye on her?

He had to know more.

The only way Roy could move around his room was if he turned off the closet light. So, he crawled over and flicked off the switch next to the door. He frog-walked over to the far side of his desk and peeked through the gap between the curtain and the wall. No way she could see him now, he reassured himself.

But she was still there, standing under the big tree and staring up at Roy's window. What was she doing?

Roy adjusted his binoculars and got a good look at

her. Even in the dark, he could see just a hint of pink on her pants. As for the strange hat, sunglasses, and gloves, they were nowhere to be found. The light on the porch illuminated half of her face. She was smiling and still aiming her binoculars right at his window.

Then she did something really bizarre. She waved and covered her mouth, seeming to hide a giggle.

Roy ducked behind his desk. Was she waving at him? What was so funny, and how could she possibly see him? Was she laughing at him for being such a crummy spy? Maybe she was a spy and knew that the first rule of spying from a window at night was that you always turned off all the lights.

Roy crawled over to his bed and lay down. Had becoming a middle-schooler made him careless and clumsy?

He slipped both hands between his head and the pillow and reminded himself of his summer with Bart again. It had been the best time of his life, and he had been the best Roy of his life. But where was that Roy now? The stealthy one? The confident one? The smart one?

A girl that he didn't even know was laughing at him for doing something he thought he was better at doing than most kids his age. What was happening to him?

Typically, girls didn't laugh at him until they had at least met him.

Roy thought about his next move.

He had nothing.

His brain felt like dry and lumpy mashed potatoes that no amount of gravy could salvage. For some reason, girls had been doing that a lot to Roy lately. Every time he was around one, his brain and mouth tangled up more than Christmas lights shoved into a too-small box.

During math class, Kristina Klaus, a girl almost anyone would think of as pretty, had asked Roy how to do a problem—a word problem Roy could do in his sleep. But when he leaned in to help her, his brain worked the problem while his mouth stuttered in some language only a doofus would understand. After about a minute of Roy's rambling, Kristina looked at him and said, "That's okay, I'll ask someone else." She turned her back to him and looked at her friend and giggled, just like the pink pants girl had done.

Roy rolled onto his side. Enough with girls, he thought. He sat up and shook his head. He felt his brain working again, so he came up with a plan.

Girls couldn't giggle at him if he stayed away from them. So, that was his plan—to stay away from them as much as possible—and that included the pink pants girl.

Roy settled in under the covers. The house across the street no longer interested him. Maybe the new neighbors were people Roy should be spying on, or maybe they were just weird. Either way, he didn't care, and he didn't want to meet any of them.

CHAPTER 4

WHATEVER.

Roy woke up the next morning to the annoying sound of his sister running down the hall and plowing through his door.

"Get up, Roy." She shook him. "We gotta go meet the neighbors. Everyone's tired of waiting for you."

Roy rolled over and faced the wall. "Get outta here, Melonie. I'm not going."

"You have to go. Mom said so and told me to get you up." She slammed her foot on his bed. "What's your problem anyway? You going through fewperty or something? Mom told me all about it. And that you might be grumpy and want to be left alone a lot. Mom's right—you're changing—but not in a good way."

Roy kicked his sister's foot off the bed. "Just tell Mom I don't feel good . . . my stomach hurts."

Melonie stomped out of his room. "Your stomach always hurts. You're no fun anymore. I hope I never go through fewperty."

Roy let out a big moan. He knew this situation was far from over, and by the time his mom entered his room, he had already accepted the fact that he was going to have to meet that girl.

"Roy, what's wrong?" His mom placed her hand on his forehead. "We're waiting for you to get ready so that we can meet the neighbors."

Roy rubbed his eyes. "My stomach hurts."

"Well, it shouldn't take long, and I don't want to go without you. Especially since they might have a child around your age." She looked out his window in the direction of the tiny house. "I think that might be really good for you. Throw some clothes on and come downstairs. Getting up and moving around should make your tummy feel better." She switched on his room light, which always signaled to Roy that he'd better not keep his mom waiting. "You shouldn't have had all those cookies. You've always had a sensitive stomach."

Roy grumbled as he crawled out of bed and didn't stop grumbling until he met everyone in the kitchen. The basket was still sitting in the middle of the table.

The vision of all the goodies was making him hungry, but he didn't dare grab anything to eat. No one eats when their stomach hurts—especially when they're pretending.

The family left out the side door and crossed the street to the neighbor's house. The cool, windy morning reminded Roy that his favorite holiday, Halloween, was less than a couple of weeks away.

Melonie ran ahead of everyone and pushed the doorbell button at least three times.

"Melonie," her mom said, running onto the porch and pulling her arm away. "Don't be rude. One time is plenty."

All the Winklesteens stood on the porch and listened to the commotion on the other side of the door. Roy heard a high-pitched voice. He knew exactly whose it was.

The door popped open, and the neighbors' three bodies blocked Roy's view from seeing anything inside. His parents proclaimed in unison, "WELCOME. We're your neighbors . . . from across the street."

Roy's dad pointed behind him. "The blue house," he said. Then he held out his hand. "I'm Charles Winklesteen, and this is my wife, Helen."

Melonie wriggled her way in front. "I'm Melonie.

This basket's for you."

The lady took the basket and smiled. "How wonderful . . . thank you so much. I'm Celia Moore, and this is my husband, Andy." She tapped the arm of the dark-framed glasses man.

Roy stood slightly behind his mom. He and the pink pants girl, who was now wearing slightly worn jeans, stared each other down. Like last night, she wasn't wearing the strange outfit he had first seen her in.

"This is Roy." His mom put her hands on his shoulders and pushed him face-to-face with the girl.

"This is Mizuki," Mrs. Moore said. "But we call her Suki."

"You mean like spooky?" Melonie asked. "That's kind of—"

"What a lovely name . . . so unique," Helen Winklesteen said, followed by an apologetic chuckle.

Mrs. Moore looked at Roy. "Suki is twelve. How old are you, Roy?"

Roy was about to speak, but Melonie beat him to it. "He's eleven. But he looks really young for his age. A man at the grocery store thought he was only nine."

"Did not, Mel." Roy flicked his sister's arm, never taking his eyes off the girl.

"Please, come in," Mr. Moore said, stepping back out

of the doorway and eyeing the basket. "That looks delicious."

"There're gummy worms in it," Melonie couldn't resist pointing out. "Mrs. Moore, did you adopt any other girls—like one who's seven?"

Suki gave Melonie a confident smirk. "Nope, I'm the only kid they've got. I'm all they need."

Helen Winklesteen cupped Melonie's chin with her hand as though poised to cover her daughter's mouth at any second. "She's so excited to meet you. She helped put the basket together."

"Melonie, why don't you come into the kitchen with me and your mom, and you can show me all the great stuff in the basket," Mrs. Moore said.

Mr. Moore and Roy's dad disappeared out the back door and into the overgrown yard. They acted like they were long-lost high school friends that hadn't seen each other in years. There was something about dads, yards, and tools that seemed to inspire instantaneous friendships.

Roy and Suki were left alone in the dingy wallpapered entry hall, still staring each other down.

Although Melonie was the rudest person Roy knew, she had made a fairly obvious assumption. Clearly, Suki was adopted. Her parents were pale, light-haired, and light-eyed.

Suki was not.

Her hair was straight and so black that it looked almost blue under the dusty light fixture, and her eyes were darker than Roy's. Her chin came to his forehead, and she was skinnier than Melonie.

"Wanna see my room?" She tilted her head toward a door down a box-filled hall.

Roy shrugged. "Whatever."

He followed Suki into the only room that looked moved into. The house was extra dark for such a sunny day. But that was because all the curtains were closed again, and the rooms were jammed packed with all the items from yesterday's move.

Suki sat on the bed. "You like fossils?"

"They're okay, I guess." Roy looked around the room for any hint of the weird outfit she had worn the day before. The space reminded him of Melonie's room, minus a couple of frills. "What does that mean?" Roy pointed to a decorative, wooden hanging piece on her wall that looked like writing from the other side of the world. "Is that Chinese or something?"

"That's my name." Suki went over to the piece and pointed to each character. "Mizuki. It means 'beautiful moon.' And it's not Chinese, it's Japanese." Suki crossed her arms. "Why is every Asian person always called Chinese? Do you know that there are at least 11 large countries considered Asian? I guess you think we all look the same, so you can call us all Chinese."

Roy took a step back from Suki. "Geez . . . sorry. I-I guess I never really thought about it. I didn't know being called Chinese was bad."

"Don't be ridiculous." Suki opened her closet door. "There's nothing wrong with being Chinese. But I'm not Chinese, so why would I be okay with being called that?"

"I guess you shouldn't be okay with being called that." Roy started backing up toward the door. His stomach was actually beginning to hurt. "I'm gonna go find my mom."

"Wait . . ." Suki placed a shoebox she had retrieved from her closet on her bed. It looked like some type of arts and crafts project that she had probably done in school to show off her hobbies. From what Roy could tell, she had a lot of interests. "Don't leave." She took the top off and slid the box toward Roy. "You said you wanted to see my fossils. Here they are."

Roy stood in the doorway. He didn't care about her name or her fossils. But there was something about this girl that kept him from running out of the room. What had she been doing in her front yard at 11 at night with binoculars? Who was she spying on? And why was she dressed so funny when he first saw her? Why close the curtains during the day and open them at night?

Roy's long list of questions begged him to stay. So, he did.

"I've been collecting them for as long as I can remember. This box is for my most special ones," Suki said.

Roy looked down. He assumed she expected him to pay attention to what she was saying. Fossils were okay, but they weren't his favorite. Plus, if he was going to stay and put up with her, he really wanted his questions answered. But he didn't want to be rude, so he acted interested. "What's so special about these?"

"They're from all the places I have lived. They're kinda like my memories."

"You've lived in a bunch of places?" Roy sat down on the floor and picked up a particularly large one. "Where's this from?

"Oh, that one is really special. It's from Japan."

"I guess I should know why that makes it special," Roy said, trying not to look so bored. "You sure it's Japanese?" Roy picked up a magnifying glass from the box and began studying the rock. "I don't know, I think it looks more Chinese."

"So, I guess you think you're funny now?" Suki tucked her long, shiny hair behind her ears so Roy could get a full view of her smile.

"Maybe a little." Roy moved the magnifier up and down until the view came into focus. The grayish rock with a sand-colored shell fused into its jagged surface looked like something Roy had seen at least a dozen times before.

"It's a brachiopod." Suki moved close to Roy to see the view from the magnifying glass. "My dad found it during my first trip to the beach, right after they adopted me."

Roy squinted and tried to look intrigued. Had it been a dinosaur bone, he wouldn't have had to fake it.

Suki continued to tell the story of how the Moores became her parents. He sort of listened and managed to pick up on the most important facts: Her dad was killed in an accident when she was a baby. Mr. Moore had worked with her father on a dig in Japan, and they had become good friends. Suki's dad had asked the Moores to be her guardians, so they adopted her after her dad died.

She didn't mention her mother.

No doubt it was a sad story, and Roy wasn't sure

how to respond, so he pretended even more interest in her fossils. "Where are some of the others from?" Roy combed his hand through the rocks.

"This one is from Morocco and this one I found in our backyard in Argentina. This one is from when we lived in China, and this one is from our last place in New Zealand."

Roy looked up from the box. He couldn't believe what he was hearing. She kept going and going—grabbing pieces of earth from all around the world—each with its own unique story. She had been everywhere—even places Roy had never heard of. Like Nangetty—where in the world was that?

Roy kept the focus on her, hoping she wouldn't ask about all the places he hadn't lived or visited. "Why have you lived so many places?"

"My dad goes on digs all around the world. He's a paleontologist. But he's retired, and now he teaches at the college. My mom teaches there too."

"He doesn't look old enough to be retired."

"Yeah." Suki began packing the box back up. "He's not old, but my mom was sick of traveling, and she didn't think it was best for me. You know, she thought we needed to settle down as a family so that I could live a normal life."

Roy's ears perked up. "Do you want to live a normal life? Because that's what I live, and trust me, it's not that much fun. Kind of boring if you ask me."

"I liked traveling. But my mom worries about me."

"Yeah . . . my mom worries too," Roy said. "I guess that's what you do when you're a mom—worry. But it's kind of annoying."

"Are you kidding me? I'm all for being normal," Suki said. "Even though I never will be."

"What's that supposed to mean?"

"How come you haven't asked me why I was out so late last night?" Suki returned the box to the closet.

Roy started feeling a little flustered. He was supposed to be asking the questions. "Um . . . it's none of my business."

"Do binoculars help you stay out of other people's business?" Suki gave him a sarcastic sneer. "Because mine don't."

Roy could feel his cheeks burning. "I wasn't looking at you. I heard something—a dog barking. So, I thought I'd check it out. You know . . . in case it was lost or something."

"Huh." Suki closed the closet and sat back down next to Roy. "I could've sworn you were looking right at my house. And I don't remember hearing a dog bark."

"Well . . . I heard it, and I wasn't looking at your house. Besides, what were you looking at?"

"At first, I was looking at the sky. Jupiter was very close to the moon and easy to spot. But then I saw you looking out your window—clear as day." She giggled. "You really should turn your light off if you are going to spy on people."

"I wasn't spying." Roy stood up and walked toward her door again.

"It's no big deal." Suki followed him and shut her door. "I like spying too."

"Whatever." Roy rolled his eyes, worried and a little curious about why she had shut her door.

"Do you still want me to answer your question?" she asked.

"What . . . about being normal?"

"No . . . about all the fossils you seem to care so little about." She gave him a fake smile. "Yeah . . . about being normal."

What was with this girl? Why was she trying to make him feel so stupid? Roy felt a hint of bravery seep through his veins, and the questions began tumbling out of his mouth. "Fine, what's not normal about you? And how come your parents let you hang out in the

"Bring your binoculars, just in case that dog barks again."

Roy smirked and joined his parents. Suki giggled as she closed her bedroom door.

CHAPTER 5

HUH?

The Winklesteens trotted back across the street to their home, where everyone fell into their typical Sunday routine. For Roy, that meant hanging out in his room and doing homework. He had plenty to do, but he couldn't concentrate.

He looked out the window at Suki's house. He couldn't figure out if the girl he had met earlier was annoyingly odd or strangely wonderful. Sure, she was bossy and loved making a fool of him, and he had no intention of being her friend, but he did find her fascinating. To Roy, she was sort of like roller coasters. He found all their hair-raising twists, heights, and hills mathematically mesmerizing, yet he would never choose to experience one.

What did she mean by wanting to be "normal?" She

looked normal. In fact, she was kind of pretty, but Roy would keep that to himself. So what if she was adopted and didn't look like her parents? Roy knew lots of kids like that.

Nope, Roy thought. There was much more to learn about his new neighbor, and he was determined to get some answers.

It was time to use the fire escape, something he hadn't thought about since the last night he had come home from Bart's. When they were younger, he and his best friend, Nicholas, used to use the rope all the time, even though his parents had installed it for the sole purpose of escaping a fire.

But since school had started, Nicholas preferred to use the front door. For some reason, he thought being a middle-schooler made all the fun, secretive activities kids did to disobey their parents seem silly, and he thought there were much more grown-up ways to prove you didn't always have to abide by your parents' rules. In a way, Roy wasn't surprised by Nicholas's newfound attitude. He had always been the more mature, outspoken one. Nicholas was the cool soccer player who made friends easily, and Roy was the klutzy dreamer with the big brain; together, they navigated life pretty well.

However, it did get a little nippy in his best friend's shadow.

But Nicholas wasn't around now, and Roy liked using the fire escape—especially at night.

Roy finished his homework and let his parents tuck him in at his regular bedtime. When 10:45 p.m. flashed on his watch, he popped out of bed, put on his clothes from earlier that day, and hung his binoculars around his neck. He made sure every light in his room was off before looking out his window.

He saw no signs of Suki.

But like him, she was a spy and knew better than to be wandering around in full view. After all, he had not seen her the first time he'd looked at her house last night. He only saw her when she wanted him to see her.

That was how spies operated.

Roy cracked his bedroom door and peered down the long dark hall toward the other bedrooms. Roy smiled. He seemed to like his family the most when they were sleeping.

Roy opened his corner bedroom window and stepped up on the sill. He gripped the branch of the hearty oak tree and spotted the thick rope. It was just as he had left it two months ago. He unwound it from around the branch and shimmied his way down to the leaf-covered grass.

He smiled. Felt like old times, he thought.

Roy crept around to the front of his house and checked for cars. He still didn't see Suki and knew she was hiding. He could feel her staring at him.

When he got to her yard, he looked behind the tree trunk she had been standing next to the night before. She wasn't there.

Had she made a fool of him again? He should've known better than to trust her. She was probably watching him—laughing.

After tiptoeing around the yard for a few more minutes, Roy gave up and turned back toward his house. *Rustle... rustle... thump.* Roy felt a wisp of air pass on the right side of his body and a vibration under his feet.

"BOO."

Roy jumped back and almost tripped on a protruding tree root.

There was Suki, laughing at him. "Scared ya," she whispered, giving him a light punch on his arm. "A good spy always knows to look up. Trees make great hiding spots."

"Ha...ha...you're so funny." Roy backed away from her.

"I know," she said. "And smart too."

Roy blew off her know-it-all attitude. He had one thing on his mind: answers. "So . . . I'm here," he said. "You've got something to tell me?"

"Not here." Suki pulled Roy's sleeve. "C'mon, follow me."

They walked past the garage door and between the houses, through the gate and into the backyard. "Watch your step." Suki marched through the tall grass. "It's a jungle back here. No one's mowed it in a year."

"So that's why you hang out in the front yard?"

"Yeah, Dad said he'll take care of it tomorrow." Suki marched to a small, white shed in the corner of the yard that desperately needed painting. "I don't care about the yard, though." She opened the worn, wooden door. "The best part of this whole house is this. I begged my dad to buy this place just so I could make this mine."

She picked up a flashlight next to the door and panned the light back and forth across the small room with walls that looked like they were still under construction. The flashlight kept flickering, so Suki tapped it against her open hand to get it to work. "It's going to be my lab, just like my grandmother used to have."

Roy looked around. The room didn't look like anything special to him. In fact, it was kind of gross with spiderwebs and dead bugs lying about and an odor that seemed to combine the worst of every smell Roy could think of. Except for a few boxes that read "Suki storage space," the place was mostly empty.

"Why do you need a lab when you have your own room?" Roy asked.

"Because . . . I need to experiment. And I can't do that in a room with carpet and frilly curtains. "Here." Suki pushed a three-legged stool his way. "Sit on this."

She dragged an old milk crate across the grimy floor and sat near Roy. They both tried to make themselves comfortable. She stood the flashlight up between them on the floor.

Experiment? Roy wondered. What did a twelve-year-old girl need to experiment on? He couldn't wait any longer. "Are you allowed to be out here . . . at night?" he asked.

"Well . . . not now." Suki sighed. "Dad thinks it's too dangerous, so he wants to fix it up for me. You know, make it safe. That's what they do with every place I've lived."

"Like your room?" Roy asked.

"Exactly. Mom and Dad spent all day yesterday

helping me set it up." She chuckled. "We are still getting our dishes out of boxes, but Suki's room is perfect and safe . . . in a little boring house . . . in a little boring neighborhood . . . in a little boring town. I'm so tired of being safe."

Safe from what? Roy wondered.

"So, I guess you want answers."

"Why else would I be here?" Roy said. "You're the one that made it sound like you have such an abnormal life—even though it looks pretty normal to me."

"Well . . . my parents, especially my mom, work very hard at making it look that way. But I'm not normal."

"So . . . what is it? What's wrong with you?"

"I have Xeroderma Pigmentosum, or XP, as most people call it," she said, rubbing her bare arm.

"What's that?" Roy didn't know whether to back away from her or be intrigued.

"It's not some big secret like you think it is. It's just a rare skin disorder I was born with." Suki brought the flashlight to her face. "Basically, it means my skin can't handle any UV rays—you know, like the sun puts out. There are only about 350 people in the United States that have it."

"I thought UV rays were bad for everyone. That's why my mom makes me wear so much sunscreen."

"Yeah . . . but my skin is super sensitive to them. Sunscreen is not nearly enough." Suki pushed back her long hair and shined the light on the right side of her neck. "See this scar?

Roy leaned toward her and studied the illuminated spot. "Yeah, it looks like a scar I have on my knee from when I fell off my bike."

"I didn't fall. It's where I had skin cancer removed when I was eight."

"Whoa . . . you were only eight?"

Suki moved her hair back over the scar. "That's why my mom is so protective of me and worries all the time."

"That explains all the stuff you were wearing."

"Yep . . . it's the only way I can be in the sun."

"Huh . . . that's why you are out at night and why all the curtains are closed during the day," Roy mumbled, glad that he hadn't offered his witness protection theory. "So, your parents know you're out at night?"

"For the most part." Suki got up and aimed her binoculars out the single tiny window facing her house. "My parents get up early and go to bed early, which is why they wanted to live in a small town that is safe. It's cool, though. I'm on my own . . . and I like it that way."

"Yeah . . . me too," Roy said.

"Why are you up?" Suki asked. "Shouldn't you be in bed right now—with tomorrow being a school day and all?"

"I'm supposed to be in bed. But my parents are daylifers too . . . and I'm not, so I can pretty much do whatever I want after they go to sleep."

"Anything?" Suki didn't look convinced.

"You know what I mean. Like you, I'm on my own at night . . . and I like it that way." Roy felt like he was being interrogated. "Except . . . my parents don't know I'm up late. They think I go to bed when they do."

"Why do you like the night? You got something wrong with you too?"

"No . . . but I do think I was born to like the nights . . . like, in my genes. I've never liked mornings. I like the moon."

Suki jumped up with the flashlight and shuffled to the door. "The moon . . . let's see if the clouds have cleared. It should be a full one tonight."

Roy followed her. He had never thought about using his binoculars to look at the sky. Stars and planets were interesting, but he found people more fun to watch. Things in the sky didn't care whether you were looking at them or not, and they were very predictable. People, on the other hand, acted one way when they knew they were being watched and a completely different way when they thought no one was paying attention to them.

Suki and Roy high-legged it through the long grass and made it back to the front yard. They both got comfortable under the tree. "Good . . . you can see it now," Suki whispered while studying the view through her binoculars.

Roy looked up too. The moon was big and bold. Its cool-blue light illuminated the top of a large cluster of clouds so that they looked more like a raging ocean than a suspended mass of water droplets and ice crystals.

"What do you have against the sun? What's it ever done to you?" Suki asked as she wiped the lenses on her binoculars with the bottom of her shirt. "Seems like I should be the one to hate it. Remember this?" She flung her hair back and rubbed her scar. "I love the sunlight . . . but it doesn't love me. I would do anything to be able to go outside and be around everyone else who loves mornings and days. I've always wanted to go to the beach and lay out in a bikini. It looks so exotic and relaxing."

"I thought you said you liked the nights?" Roy tried to hide his disappointment. The night wasn't turning out to be nearly as interesting as he thought it would be.

"I like days and nights. I mean, you're right, the moon is pretty cool. We would never be looking at the sun with our binoculars." Suki looked back at the sky.

For the first time in his life, Roy looked at the moon with his binoculars.

"Oh . . . I see the Copernicus crater . . . bright as ever," Suki said.

Craters? They had names? Roy turned the focus nob.

"You see it?" Suki asked.

"Uh . . . yeah," he said.

"No, you don't. Here . . . look through these." Suki handed her binoculars to Roy. "It's the white spot, on the left half of the moon, not quite half-way down."

Roy brought the much larger, heavier binoculars to his face. He scanned for the spot. "Oh . . . yeah . . . I see it."

"It's about 500 miles across," she explained. "It was named after the astronomer Nicolaus Copernicus."

Roy gave back the binoculars. "You want to be an astronomer or something?"

Suki rolled her eyes and shook her head.

"What?" Roy asked. "I mean, you seem to know a lot

about it and spend a lot of time looking at the sky."

"I know a lot about a lot of things. Astronomy is just one of them. I do want to be a scientist, though."

"Is that why you're so excited about your lab in the backyard?"

"My grandmother was a scientist. She worked for NASA. Whenever I visited her, we would spend all our time together in her lab at her house."

"Then that's why you like space and stuff?"

"Maybe... but she never really talked about it much. By the time I came around, she had retired. Besides, we spent most of our nights working on an experiment, so there wasn't much time to talk about her career."

Suki panned the sky from left to right. "Stars and planets are something I like looking at for fun. The sky is much more interesting at night, and it's the only reason humans ever figured out we live on a speck in the universe."

Roy thought for a minute. She was right. If it weren't for night, humans would still be in the dark about so many things. Roy grinned. Now he had one more reason to prefer nights to days.

"What were you doing in her lab?" Roy asked.

Suki looked around like she was afraid someone

might be listening. "It's top secret."

"Yeah . . . right."

"I'm not kidding," Suki whispered as loud as she could. "You'd have to see it to actually believe what my grandmother created. It's that amazing and important."

"I won't tell anyone," Roy said, looking around too.

"I'm not about to tell you." Suki got up and walked toward a door on the side of her house. "I hardly know you. And most of the kids I know can't keep a secret to save their life."

"Are you kidding me?" Roy said. "I can keep a secret . . . better than anyone I know—even better than old people."

"That's what anyone would say." Suki opened the door. "You'd better go home. You have to go to school, remember?"

"You do too. Isn't that why my mom made me meet you, so you would know someone on your first day?"

"I don't go to school. I learn from home on my own while my parents work."

"Oh . . . because of your skin problem?"

"No. I could go to school. It's just that I'm a fast learner and way ahead of most kids my age. Besides, I got tired of changing schools every time we moved to a new place. But I've thought about going to school. I don't know . . . maybe I will . . . someday."

"Huh" was all Roy could say. He had never met a kid smarter than him, and he wasn't sure how he felt about it.

Suki gave Roy a sort of disgusted look. "Still, if I did go to school, I wouldn't need anyone to hold my hand. I can get by just fine on my own."

"I wouldn't hold your hand," Roy said with a more disgusted look back.

"Good," Suki huffed back. "Same time tomorrow night?"

Roy scrunched his nose. "Maybe."

Suki scrunched back. "Whatever." She went inside, never looking back as she closed the door behind her.

CHAPTER 6

SERIOUSLY!

Roy made it back to his house undetected and climbed into bed. He didn't know what to think of Suki. So far, she was like a boring movie that kept promising some strange twist or reveal only to disappoint you with a lame ending after two hours of nothing.

Why did she need a lab? She was only 12. And what top-secret experiment would a NASA scientist reveal to a child—even if she was her granddaughter?

Suki seemed full of herself and enjoyed making a fool out of Roy. How dare she not trust him? He was the most trustworthy person on the planet. Just ask Bart. Certainly, his secret was much more fantastic than anything she had to offer.

She was no more a spy, a famous person, or a witness to a crime than he was. Okay, she had some skin disorder that forced her to stay out of the sun—big deal. It didn't sound so bad to Roy. She could get up whenever she wanted. She could do her schoolwork whenever she wanted. She could stay up as late as she wanted, and she had loads of freedom to do what she wanted. She probably got gifts when it wasn't her birthday or a holiday—all because of her disorder.

She wasn't even a real nightlifer. Although Roy had to admit that she had made an excellent point: the night sky was much more interesting than the day sky. How could he have never realized that? Maybe true nightlifers automatically knew stuff like that and had no need to dwell on the obvious.

That must have been it, Roy thought. Suki wasn't smarter than him; she only pointed out things he wasn't aware he already knew.

He buried his head in his pillow and closed his eyes. He wasn't sure about meeting Suki tomorrow night.

He'd have to think about it.

Roy had an especially hard time getting out of bed that morning. He barely noticed Nicholas slide in next to him on the bus and almost forgot why he had recently grown to hate the morning rides to school.

But as the worst stop in the neighborhood came into view, his memory kindly reminded him it was time for certain feelings to cut to the front of the line. Dread wrapped its slimy tentacles so tight around Roy that he felt like he couldn't breathe.

Shaaaaaaroooosh. The bus door slapped open, and there it stood, his giant, sloppy middle-grade problem, looking eager to torture anything in its path. It *plomped* up the steps and eclipsed the view out the front window as it turned to make its way down the aisle.

The entire bus went silent.

Plomp, plomp, plomp. It swayed by the rows of seats, staring down anyone that dared to look into its eyes. Roy shifted his stare out the window. But he knew it didn't matter. It, or Blob, as Roy preferred to think of him, was heading his way.

Roy caught a glimpse of the immense, bulging nightmare before him. He could see two chest hairs peeking over the stretched collar of Blob's stained t-shirt. This guy had to have flunked about five grades. Chest hairs—seriously? What eighth-grader has chest hairs? The only noticeable hair Roy had was on his head. Blob looked like he should have been driving the bus, not tormenting a smart sixth-grader who tested into an eighth-grade algebra class.

"Move it," Blob said, gesturing to the kid sitting directly behind Roy. The kid didn't hesitate. He shimmied out of the seat and relocated to the back somewhere.

"Here we go again," Nicholas mumbled through his still lips. Roy could sense the frustration in his best friend's words. Who could blame him? This was all his fault. If Roy had never gotten the highest grade on the math test last week, then Blob would have never given Roy a second glance.

Blob squeezed his linebacker frame onto the seat behind Roy. His minion, Rob, slid in beside him. Roy and Nicholas looked straight ahead.

Roy felt a finger flick to the back of his neck. "Hey, Tinkleweenie, hand it over," Blob said. "You know the drill."

Over the years, Roy's last name had inspired many amusing monikers: Twinklesteen, Wonkysteen (Roy was kind of clumsy), and Frank-n-bean, to name a few. But Tinkleweenie was, by far, the most embarrassing.

Nicholas turned around and gave Blob his most threatening glare. "Leave him alone. Do your own homework."

Roy could hear his heart beating over the roaring bus engine. This was going to be bad.

Blob forced his face in between the two friends. "Hey, Tinkleweenie, tell your girlfriend to shut up."

Rob laughed and gave Roy a flick too. "Better do what he says."

Nicholas stared both of them down as Roy lifted his backpack into his lap and unzipped it. As much as Roy appreciated Nicholas's sixth-grade confidence and unwavering bravery, he wished his best friend would keep his mouth shut.

"Whatta you lookin' at?" Blob snarled at Nicholas.

Roy could feel Nicholas's eyes shift his way. His stare said it all. His best friend thought he was a coward—a wimp—a loser. But for the time being, Roy didn't care. He just wanted the situation to end.

Roy pulled his notebook out and handed it to Blob.

Blob snatched it and patted Roy on the head. "Good boy," he said. He leaned back in the seat and ripped through the notebook until he found the latest assignment. "These all better be right."

Nicholas looked back at the two eighth-graders scrawling down the answers and laughing. "Stupid," he muttered.

"You say somethin'?" Blob leaned forward and got so

close to Nicholas that Roy could smell his unbrushed mouth. "You better keep your girlfriend in line, Tinkleweenie. I'd hate to have to hurt her."

Rob laughed and said, "You kiddin' me? You live to hurt."

"Wouldn't even break a sweat." Blob shifted back next to Rob and kicked the back of the seat behind Nicholas, and then the two finished up their copying.

Blob tossed the notebook between Roy and Nicholas right as the bus came to a stop in front of the school. The brakes on the bus let out their typical high-pitched squeak, which signaled everyone to gather up their packs, line up in the aisle, and head to the door.

Blob and Rob pushed their way between some kids. Roy was still loading his notebook into his pack, so Nicholas waited beside him. The door swooshed open, and everyone began to move. Nicholas stood up and stepped toward the line.

Blob stretched out his arm around the two kids in front of him and pushed Nicholas back. "You ain't gettin' in front of me—loser. You sit your girly butt back down."

Nicholas retreated and almost sat down on Roy's lap. Roy couldn't tell if Nicholas was shaking from fear, anger, or both.

As Blob lumbered his way past their seat, Nicholas couldn't hold back any longer. He stuck his foot out right in time to snag Blob's untied tennis shoe. Blob's back arched, and his arms flailed. He fell into Rob, and then Rob fell into the girl in front of him, and so on. The line of kids became a row of bumping dominoes, only stopping when the kid at the front was able to grab onto the metal pole at the stairs.

Blob teetered back onto his feet. He grabbed Nicholas's backpack strap and pulled him toward his face. "You're dead—loser." Blob pulled his other arm back, clenched his fist, and took aim right for Nicholas's face.

"Hey . . . what's goin' on back there?" The bus driver stood up and pointed right at Blob. "Whadda you think you're doin'?"

"This ain't over." Blob released the strap and pushed Nicholas into Roy. "I know where you live. If I were you, I'd grow eyes in the back of my head." Blob walked down the aisle and out the door, keeping his glare on Nicholas as much as possible.

Fortunately, the bus driver never took his eyes off Blob and offered him some words of advice as he stepped onto the stairs. "Keep your bad attitude off my bus."

Roy and Nicholas scrambled to catch up to the end of the line. "You, okay?" the bus driver asked as Nicholas passed by.

Nicholas nodded, keeping his head down. Roy gave the bus driver a big smile. It was the least he could do, given the fact that the gruff-looking old man had saved his best friend's life.

"C'mon . . . hurry," Roy said, tugging on Nicholas's pack. They shuffled toward the sixth-grade wing. Roy let out a sigh of relief as they settled into their first-period desks. Most mornings, they would hang around outside and talk with friends, but considering the event that had just unfolded, Roy wanted to lay low.

"What are we going to do?" Roy's voice was shaky as he turned to his friend, rummaging through his backpack.

"About what?" Nicholas asked.

"You know . . . he wants to kill you. He almost punched you."

"Who cares?" Nicholas huffed. "He's not going to kill me. He's all talk and testosterone. And if he hit me . . . I'd swing back . . . that's for sure. Besides, the bus driver can't stand him, and he's not going to let him get away with beating someone up."

"Yeah, the bus driver seems to really hate him," Roy

said. "We should get that seat right behind him."

"That girl always sits there," Nicholas reminded him. "And I don't like sitting at the front of the bus anyway—it's boring up there."

Roy couldn't argue with Nicholas. The front of the bus was where all the quiet kids seemed to sit. But he could use a good dose of boring.

Roy had already made up his mind. He didn't care what Nicholas wanted. The minute the dismissal bell rang, he was taking off for the buses, and he was claiming that front seat behind the driver.

"Stop giving him your homework," Nicholas commanded as he pulled out his English book. "Giving in to him just makes things worse—for everyone."

"It's easy for you to say that." Roy felt a worry headache coming on. "You don't have a class with him and a bunch of other eighth-graders. I'm the only sixth-grader that goes into the eighth-grade wing—and that's only because I have to."

"Still... he's nothing but a pile of muscle and anger. He only has friends because everyone is too afraid not to be his friend. You're smart, and all the other eighth-graders know it. Going to the eighth-grade wing could be cool... if you played it right. If you stood up for yourself, everybody else would respect you and want to hang out with you."

Roy looked away. He couldn't bear seeing the angry look on his friend's face. "I don't know. It's easy to say that when you're safe in the sixth-grade wing."

Nicholas lowered his voice as the other kids piled into the classroom. "Make friends with some of the other kids in the class, and maybe they'll help you out. Aren't there some in your math class that ride our bus?"

"Maybe . . . I don't know."

As more kids entered the classroom, excitement filled the air. A bunch of kids gathered around Nicholas. One even sat on Roy's desk. The news was spreading fast—Nicholas had stood up to the biggest, meanest jock in school.

One kid asked, "How much did he bleed when you punched him?"

Another kid chimed in, "I heard you hit him so hard in the gut that he puked."

Roy couldn't believe it. Nicholas was some sort of hero. The rest of the kids couldn't get enough of him, and the information they had was more made up than Melonie after she raided his mom's cosmetic drawer.

"Did the bus driver really kick you off because you hit that guy so hard?" the most popular kid in the sixth grade asked.

Roy looked at Nicholas. His friend had the biggest grin on his face—bigger than anything Roy had ever seen before. He was just sitting there, listening to all the ridiculous stories, and not correcting one of them.

"I can't believe you beat him up," the kid sitting on Roy's desk said. "What did he do to you?"

Nicholas looked at Roy. Roy looked at Nicholas. Neither one of them wanted the truth to be told. That was obvious. So, Nicholas didn't say much. "He's a jerk," he said. "He scares everyone into being his friend or doing what he wants . . . and he's mean just to be mean . . . and we shouldn't let him get away with it."

Roy sat quietly at his desk watching the kids hover around Nicholas like he was some sort of superhero that had leaped right out of a comic book. He wasn't sure how he felt about Nicholas playing along with all the outlandish stories. But he was glad his best friend had kept the real reason to himself.

Roy wondered. Would Nicholas have been that brave if it were his homework Blob had demanded? Nicholas didn't have to worry about getting along with eighth-graders—but Roy did—and he was pretty sure that they weren't interested in preposterous rumors about how a sixth-grader beat up the toughest kid in school.

CHAPTER 7

WHEW.

Roy had math right before lunch, which was good, considering the school meals often made him nauseous. His heart and head were pounding as he entered the eighth-grade wing.

Roy saw Rob standing at the door to the math class. Mrs. Crowley stopped talking to Rob and looked right at Roy as he walked over. "Good morning, Roy," she said with her typical wrinkled smile. "Great job on the quiz last Friday. You made the highest score."

Roy forced a smile back and avoided eye contact with Rob. He slid by both of them and hurried to his desk. He looked around the room filled with bigger kids, bigger conversations, and bigger complications. Roy felt small, immature, and simple. So what if he was great at math? Algebra was the only thing about eighth grade that he could figure out. He didn't belong there, and he knew all the other kids felt the same way.

To Roy's relief, Blob was nowhere to be found.

He was safe for now, and like he thought, no one was talking about the bus incident. Eighth-graders couldn't care less about sixth-graders. Making friends with them, as Nicholas had suggested, was about as likely as Roy growing chest hairs any time soon.

When Roy met up with his grade for lunch, everyone was still buzzing about Nicholas. Roy continued to keep his mouth shut. He saw no advantage to anyone knowing the truth and doubted whether anyone cared about the truth anyway. Plus, Roy had bigger concerns on his mind, like getting the seat behind the bus driver so Nicholas could live to see Tuesday.

As soon as the bell gave its final shout-out for the day, Roy flung his pack across one shoulder and sprinted out the door. He dodged in between all the chattering groups of kids and headed toward the circular drive at the front of the school.

After spotting bus 5522 down at the end of the line, he changed his course slightly and made it through the door before anyone else. Roy offered another smile to the driver before taking the seat behind him. The driver looked in the mirror and grinned back.

Roy was relieved. He had been worried that the driver might tell him to move because the girl who typically sat there had a little trouble walking. Just in case, Roy tossed his backpack on the seat right behind the steps. The girl could have that seat. It was just as close to the door.

Roy watched everyone load onto the bus. He caught a glimpse of Nicholas surrounded by kids still begging to know more about his big fight with Blob. It was official—Nicholas was becoming a popular kid. In fact, he was so busy talking to some other sixth-graders that he almost passed right by Roy.

"Hey . . . Nicholas . . . we're right here." Roy pointed to the open space next to him.

Nicholas turned around, glanced at Roy, and then turned back toward the other kids gesturing for him to sit with them. Nicholas looked at Roy. "Really . . . the first seat?" he said. "What about that girl?"

"She can sit here." Roy looked at his backpack. Nicholas gazed at the back of the bus.

"C'mon, Nick. Back here," one kid shouted.

Nicholas waved at the kids in the back. "Thanks . . . I got a space." He slid in next to Roy.

The girl came up behind Nicholas. She stopped and stared at both of them.

"Hey... I saved you a seat." Roy pointed to his right. Nicholas took the pack and tossed it in Roy's lap. "It's closer to the steps. I thought it might be a better seat for you."

The girl smiled at Roy and took the seat.

"We look like wimps sitting up here," Nicholas said. "That kid's not even going to be on the bus. He got suspended or something."

"Oh... well... it's not that bad up here. It'll be quicker to get off."

Nicholas didn't look at Roy. "Whatever... you shouldn't be so afraid of everything."

Roy panicked. He knew he wasn't afraid of everything. This past summer had proven that. But what good was his summer adventure if no one knew about it? Everyone else still thought he was the same sheltered boy he had always been, and apparently, Nicholas was growing tired of it.

The only thing scarier than sticking up to a bully was losing your best friend.

Roy faked a chuckle. "Yeah... that guy is the loser—not us. I don't know what I was thinking. I guess... you know... a new school and all... and having to be with the eighth-graders. But they think I'm pretty cool." Roy squirmed a little. "I mean, I got the highest grade on the last quiz and didn't even brag about it. Some of the kids are even asking me to help them."

Roy saw a slight smile appear on Nicholas's face, so he kept on saying what he thought his friend wanted to hear. "You're right. It's easy to make friends with them. I guess I was worried for nothing." Nicholas's smile got bigger as Roy rambled on. "Sorry for making you sit in the front. I won't do it again."

Nicholas gave Roy an approving nod. "It's okay. I guess it's a big deal having to go to the eighth-grade wing. And that guy can be scary. I can't believe I tripped him." Nicholas started laughing. "He's so big . . . I thought he was going to crush everyone in the line, and they were going to have to call the fire department to rescue everyone from under him."

Roy laughed and joked with his best friend the whole way home. He was relieved that he seemed to have changed Nicholas's mind about him being afraid of everything.

Nevertheless, Roy had never been so glad to be home. He was exhausted. He got a snack and retreated to his room. His window reminded him that there was more to life than school.

Did Suki really have some top-secret information?

Roy fell back on his bed. Suki was no Bart—that was for sure. Would he meet her tonight?

Maybe. But maybe not.

CHAPTER 8

PROMISE?

Dinner at the Winklesteens' was unusually quiet that night. Roy figured it was because getting settled back into school's unforgiving routine always took a toll on everyone—even his mom—who seemed to enjoy the more laid-back times in the summer.

Regardless, Helen Winklesteen always seemed to do the right thing. "I was thinking about inviting the Moores over for a late afternoon barbecue this Saturday."

"That sounds like a good idea," Roy's dad said. "It'll be nice to enjoy the grill one last time before it gets too chilly."

"Can I invite Zoey to come over?" Melonie asked. "If Roy gets to have a friend there, then I should get to."

Friend? Roy thought. Suki wasn't his friend. Why

was everyone so determined to make this girl his friend? Roy had friends. What he wanted from Suki was answers, and he wasn't going to get that at a barbecue.

"Suki can't be in the sun," Roy butted in. "It could kill her."

Melonie forgot about her previous demand for inviting a friend over. "The sun will kill her?"

"Roy, there is no need for that kind of talk," his mom said, flashing him a frustrated look. "Mrs. Moore told me all about Suki's situation," she started to explain in her calmest tone. "She can be in the sun with proper protection. As a matter of fact, she enjoys being outside. Her mom says it's fine, and we'll get together around five-thirty to make things safer."

"But what if the sun gets to Suki and she dies?" Melonie asked, her voice cracking a little.

His dad looked utterly confused. "What are you and Roy talking about?" he asked.

"She has a skin disorder . . . it has a weird name, so she calls it XP," Roy said. "UV rays are really dangerous for her and damage her skin forever and can cause cancer. So, I don't think we should invite them. It seems mean."

"Roy, it's not mean," his mom said. "She has what

she needs to be safe. Her mother said it is nothing for us to be concerned about. She mostly doesn't like people staring and giving her strange looks. But that's the great thing about a barbecue in the backyard—there are no strangers around to stare at her. She just wants to be like everyone else."

"And we are not going to say anything to hurt Suki's feelings—are we, Melonie?" his dad asked as he looked at his daughter.

"Maybe we should bring her some more gummy worms," Melonie said. "They always make me feel good."

"We'll see. I'll call them tomorrow. It should be fun," Roy's mom said. Then she returned to eating her well-balanced meal, which signaled everyone else should do the same.

"I've got a lot of homework," Roy said. He cleared his dishes and went upstairs. He'd had enough of the Suki conversation.

Roy spent the rest of the evening in his room. Constant glances out his bedroom window interrupted his efforts to complete his homework. Now that his entire family thought that he and Suki should be best buddies, meeting her tonight seemed much less exciting.

Roy zipped up his pack, turned off his desk lamp, drew the curtains, and got ready for bed. He was tired and wasn't convinced Suki had anything top secret to tell him. He got into bed and pulled the covers up to his nose. He was almost asleep when his dad cracked his door open and wished him a good night.

Sleep—that was what he needed. Roy closed his eyes. His body settled into the soft mattress and seemed to thank him for the rest.

But unlike his body, his mind was raring to go. It had too much to think about: Blob, homework, secrets, rumors, Suki, Blob, middle school, friends, Nicholas, Blob, fear, Nicholas, Blob, embarrassment, Blob, Blob. It was like a circus gone bonkers in his head.

He tossed and turned. Eventually, his clock read 10:28 p.m. He sat up and returned to his desk. He got his binoculars and looked straight at Suki's house. He scoured her entire yard, even focusing on the gaps between the leaf clusters on the big tree to make sure she wasn't hanging out on one of the branches.

He saw nothing. Roy didn't know what to do. Should he meet her?

He thought about it for a while and then came up with the perfect solution. He would get dressed and monitor her yard, and if she appeared, he would give her one last chance to keep him interested. But that was all she was getting.

Roy dug his clothes out of the laundry bin and waited by his window. Right as 10:50 p.m. glowed on his clock, he noticed a shadow near the side of Suki's house. He knew it had to be her, so he ducked behind his desk.

He moved around to the side and peeked through the gap between the curtain and window frame. Suki had her binoculars aimed straight at his window. Then she brought them down and waved right at him.

How did she know he was looking at her? Did she have some sort of special night-vision eyes?

He pulled open his curtains and waved back. Then he tiptoed over to his corner window and opened the sash. He slid down the rope and ran to her yard.

"You forgot your binoculars," Suki immediately pointed out as he met her under the tree. "You're not a very good spy, are you?" She let out a soft giggle. "That's okay, you can borrow mine. They're better anyway."

There she goes again, Roy thought. He hadn't even said anything, and she was already making him look bad.

"Binoculars give you away... when you're a spy."

Roy stiffened his body and stood as straight as possible, but his head still only came to about the center of her chin. "A spy should always think someone is watching. You have to be careful not to blow your cover by having spy stuff out where everyone can see it."

"In this neighborhood? At this hour?" Suki threw her hands out and looked around. "Who do you think is watching? Maybe that chipmunk that lives over there." She pointed down their street. "But that's about it. And I don't think it'll say anything."

"You do things your way, and I'll do things my way." Roy was starting to regret not staying in bed. "Besides, I didn't come over here to spy."

"Then why are you here?" Suki began walking to the side of the house. "I'm pretty sure it's not because you want to talk about astronomy."

Roy couldn't believe she was asking him that. "I came over here to find out if you were telling the truth about your grandmother's top-secret experiment." Roy followed Suki into the recently mowed backyard. "I think you're joking with me."

Suki turned around and bent at the waist so she could look right into his eyes. "I don't care what you think. I know what I know, and now that my grandmother is gone, I'm the only one that knows it."

She opened the door to the shed. "And it's so incredible that it would make the front page of every paper and be the top story on every TV news show."

"Well, it never will if you don't tell anybody . . . it's nothing . . . meaningless."

"It's not meaningless," Suki grumbled back. "It could change the world."

"In a good way or a bad way?" Roy asked. "Bad things make the front page more than good. It must be bad, or your grandmother would have told NASA about it."

Suki entered the shed, shut the door behind Roy, and whispered even more quietly than before. "It's both."

She got the flashlight from the same place as the night before and sat down on the crate. She turned it on and placed it on its end at her feet. Roy sat across from her. "What do you mean, it's both?" he asked.

"Just what it means," Suki said. "For everything good it can make happen, something bad could happen too. That's why my grandmother wanted us to keep it to ourselves—at least until she figured everything out."

Roy didn't know what to say, and he felt the less he said, the more he would hear. So, he kept things simple. "Whoa."

"Yeah, 'whoa' is right," Suki said. "My grandmother was afraid it might wind up in the wrong hands."

"If your grandmother thought it could turn out bad, then why was she working on it in the first place?"

"She wasn't working on it...it happened by accident."

CHAPTER 9

TRUST ME.

Okay, Roy could no longer deny the fact that Suki was definitely interesting. He looked around the dingy shed like he was concerned someone might hear him. He even looked over at the window to make sure no one was looking at them. Then he scooched the stool as close to Suki as he could without it feeling weird.

"What do you mean it just happened? Like some experiment gone wrong?" Roy asked. His mouth was wide open. "Like when a person goes from good to evil by drinking some secret concoction?"

"Sort of," Suki said. "But that's all I can say."

"Aw, c'mon . . . I'm not going to tell anyone."

"I can't." Suki looked down and fidgeted with the flashlight so it stopped flickering. "I promised my grandmother."

Roy knew she wanted to tell. She was about to bust. He could feel it. Just like Bart, she needed to tell someone. "You don't understand. No one is better at keeping a secret than me." He picked up the flashlight and tapped it on the concrete floor until it completely stopped flickering.

"I don't even know you, Roy Winklesteen. Why should I trust you?"

"Well . . . because . . . I have never told anyone else's secrets—and some of them are really big."

"Oh . . . yeah . . . like what?"

"Like I said . . . I can't tell, and I never will."

"Fine . . . then neither can I." Suki crossed her arms and broadened her shoulders a little.

"Then I guess I should go."

What a waste of time, Roy thought.

He stood up and stepped toward the door. As he turned, his foot knocked over the flashlight, causing it to roll near a cluster of boxes at the back of the shed. It flickered several times before completely turning off.

The full moon gave a slight cool-blue tone to the otherwise scarily-dark shed. Roy got down on his knees and desperately patted around for the flashlight. He might have preferred night to day, but he had never been a huge fan of dark places—especially in an old shed in a strange girl's backyard.

Suki felt around on the floor as well. "Way to be brilliant . . . Winklesteen."

"Got it." Roy lifted his hand to display the flashlight. He fumbled with the switch for a little while and then tapped it several times on a box nearby. The light flickered on, but the box tipped over, and all the contents spilled out across the floor. Roy aimed the light in the direction of the noise. A mess of spray bottles, paper, plastic containers, and an assortment of pens, pencils, and other small office supplies was strewn about.

"Sorry," Roy said as he began to gather up all the contents.

"Stop touching my stuff," Suki said, yanking Roy's arm away. "I'll do it. Just go . . . leave."

"I said I was sorry. What's the big deal? I knocked it over—I should pick it all up."

Roy twisted his arm from Suki's grip. He focused the light on a pile of tangled paperclips and rubber bands. "Besides, this stuff doesn't look like anything secret to me." He scooped up the cluster and placed it in an upright bin nearby.

Suki picked up the bin and threw it in the box. "I told you to leave." She collected more supplies and tossed them in the box as well.

"Fine." Roy swiveled the flashlight in his hand so the end was facing down. He tried to place it upright on the floor, but it kept falling over. He tested a different spot a few inches away.

It fell over again.

Roy illuminated the area of the floor with the light. He saw nothing but dusty concrete. He examined the end of the flashlight. Why wouldn't it stand up?

He looked at Suki, who seemed somewhat frantic to clean up the mess with or without the light. Roy swept the concrete with the side of his hand to clear the area of any tiny bits that might be throwing the flashlight off-balance.

And that's when he felt something.

Actually, he detected quite a few somethings. The objects were about the size of a quarter, except square in shape and about as thick as a typical pad of paper. They felt strangely familiar.

Roy blinked several times and shined the flashlight right where the objects should have been.

"I thought I told you to leave." Suki yanked the flashlight away from him and swiped her hand across the area where he was looking. He could hear things tumbling across the floor. "Go home, Roy . . . now." She pointed to the door with the flashlight's beam.

Roy didn't move. "What's going on? What are those things?"

"None of your business." She tried pulling Roy up, but he didn't budge. Instead, he ran both hands across the floor in a circular motion until he hit one of the objects. He pinched it between his fingers and brought it to his face.

Suki pointed the flashlight at his hand and attempted to take it from him. "Give it to me."

Roy closed his hand and put it behind his back. "No way." He twisted around and opened his hand. "At least not until you tell me what I'm holding."

Suki let out a big sigh. She dropped the flashlight on the floor and sat down on a box behind her.

She said nothing.

"Well . . . you might as well tell me because I'm not giving it back until you do." Roy squeezed the object, hoping to figure it out on his own.

"I'm such an idiot. My grandmother would be so disappointed in me."

Roy picked up the flashlight and sat down across from her. He brought his hand around and aimed the light beam right where he felt the object resting on his palm.

yard so late at night? And what's with that weird outfit I saw you in yesterday?"

The door swung open, and there stood both mothers with Melonie squished in between them.

"Suki, why was the door closed?" her mother asked, looking at Roy with semi-suspicious eyes.

"You were being loud," Suki quickly responded. "Roy and I couldn't hear each other. How do you expect us to become friends if we can't even hear each other talk?"

Roy gave Suki an agreeable glance.

"Let's go," his mom said. "The Moores need to get settled in."

The mothers and fathers met in the hallway and babbled all the way to the front door, where Melonie was waiting. Roy started to follow.

"Wait," Suki whispered. "I never answered your questions."

Roy looked at her with S-shaped eyebrows and a slightly open mouth. All he could do was shrug his shoulders.

"Can you meet me tonight . . . in my yard . . . around eleven?" she asked.

Roy looked at his parents and then shrugged his shoulders again. "No problem."

He saw absolutely nothing.

But he knew he was holding something. When he poked and squeezed it, he could hear a slight crinkling sound. He tucked the flashlight under his arm and picked up the object with his other hand.

He looked at Suki. "What . . . am . . . I . . . holding?"

"It's a Starburst." Suki yanked the object out of his hand. "You know . . . the candy."

"Yeah . . . I know what a Starburst is. But why can't I see it?"

"Because it's invisible. That's why."

"Invisible?"

"Yeah . . . you know . . . the opposite of visible." Suki peeled back the invisible wrapper and popped an orange square in her mouth.

Roy's eyes were open wide for so long that they began to burn. "You can buy Starbursts with invisible wrappers?"

"Pleeeaaaaase . . . don't be stupid," Suki said, still chewing. "I made them invisible."

CHAPTER 10

NO WAY!

Roy fell to his knees and began feeling all around on the shed floor. Suki joined in. He managed to locate two more squares and secure them in his hand. Suki found several more and dropped them in a small plastic container.

They sat across from each other with the flashlight upright between them. Roy struggled to open one of the pieces of candy. When he finally peeled back the wrapper to reveal a chewy yellow square of yumminess, Roy gasped at the sight before him.

"I told you my grandmother had invented something incredible." Suki stuffed another Starburst in her mouth. "I guess you owe me an apology."

"Yeah . . . no problem . . . sorry." Roy still couldn't believe what he was seeing—or not seeing. "You're right. Invisible candy wrappers would make the news. And I see what you mean by it being good and bad. Good for kids because they can hide it from their parents—which means parents would think it's bad . . . right?"

Suki slapped her forehead with her hand. "No . . . no. My grandmother didn't invent a way to make candy wrappers invisible. She invented a way to make almost everything invisible—even people. I just made the candy invisible so my mom wouldn't know I had taken them. It's supposed to be for Halloween, but she bought so much that I didn't think she'd miss a small bag of Starbursts." Suki reached into the container and appeared to grab another piece. "They were sitting in the container on top of the box until you had to go and make a mess of everything."

"Sorry about that." Roy laughed a little. "I never thought being such a klutz would pay off in such a big way." He examined the piece of half-unwrapped candy between his fingers.

"Yeah . . . well, you've put me in a really bad place." Suki's face dropped. "My grandmother wouldn't be happy. Now what am I supposed to do?"

"It wasn't your fault. Maybe it was meant to be." Roy had about a billion questions seeping out of every crevasse in his gray matter, and he wasn't going to leave until Suki had answered every one of them. "It's an awfully big secret for just one kid to keep."

"That's right." Suki's entire body stiffened. "You can never tell anyone. Not even if your life depends on it. Not even if you know the world is coming to an end and it won't matter if you tell." Her eyes looked like two black holes revving up to shoot laser beams at him. "Got it?"

"Don't worry about it. Like I said, I'm great at keeping secrets."

Suki snatched the yellow piece of candy from his fingers. "You'd better be."

Roy couldn't tell if Suki was angry or worried, but he didn't really care. Answers—he wanted answers. "You said it was an accident. So, she accidentally discovered a way to make things invisible? Is that what your lab is for? Are you going to—"

"Wait just a minute." Suki stood up and looked out the window toward the back of her house. "I'm not going to tell you anything more until you tell me a secret." She turned around and glared his way. "I think that's only fair . . . right?"

She certainly presented a good argument. But Roy couldn't possibly tell her about Bart.

Could he?

He wasn't sure what to say. He needed to think for a minute.

"Hello . . . earth to Roy Winklesteen." Suki waved her hand, trying to get his attention.

"Alright, I guess that's fair. Just give me a few minutes."

"It's more than fair. And it better be a good secret." Suki began tapping her foot, waiting for him to blow her mind.

Roy's heart began to pound to the beat of her taps. He needed to tell her something awesome, and his summer with Bart was just that—awesome. But the more he thought about it, the more he knew he could never tell her, or anyone. It wasn't his secret to tell. Besides, he would blow his trustworthy reputation if he did, which would defeat the purpose of proving he was trustworthy.

He would have to settle on another secret—one that was totally his—and hope it was enough to win her confidence. The only problem was all his secrets were embarrassing.

Suki sat back down and rolled her eyes. "I don't think you have a—"

"I wet the bed until I was nine." He said it so fast

that he wasn't sure she understood him.

For a few seconds, Suki sat there, staring at him. Then she hugged her belly and let out a huge laugh. She was laughing so hard that she teetered onto her back and almost fell off the box.

"Are you crazy? Keep it down," Roy demanded. "You know it's not very nice to laugh at someone who has a problem—especially one they can't control."

Suki sat back up and put her hand over her mouth.

"You should know that better than anyone." Roy gave her his ugliest snarl.

"Okay . . . I'm sorry. You're right. It's not nice to laugh." Suki's face relaxed. "Don't worry, I won't tell."

"You'd better not. Only me and my parents know about it . . . except you . . . and I'm pretty sure I shouldn't have told you."

Suki threw up her hands. "No . . . no. I promise. Your secret is safe. I get it. Besides, you're not the only one who has had that problem. It's just that . . . no one talks about it."

"That's why it's a secret," Roy reminded her. "So, is it good enough?"

Suki presented an exaggerated look of confusion. "Well . . ." She scooched in closer to Roy, almost knocking over the flashlight. "Okay . . . I'm gonna tell you everything. But remember, I know your secret, and as long as my secret is safe, yours will be too."

Roy leaned in closer to Suki as well. It felt a little weird, but there was no way he was going to miss one word of what she was about to say.

"When my grandmother, Dr. Aileen Moore, worked for NASA, she helped design spacesuits to protect astronauts from the sun's radiation." Suki rubbed her cheek as though trying to remove some of her freckles. "There's life on earth because the magnetic field and our atmosphere protect us from the sun . . . well, most of us anyway. But when you are in space, the radiation is really bad for humans," she said with a serious whisper.

Roy nodded like he understood what she was talking about.

"My grandmother knew her stuff when it came to the sun, so it only made sense that she would try to help me." Suki looked over both shoulders before continuing. "She came up with the idea to create a spray that, when dried, would act as a coating to shield me from UV rays. She wanted it to work on everything—like skin and hair and glass and clothes."

"Like a sunscreen you spray on?" Roy said. "I have some of that."

"But it would be much better than sunscreen," she explained. "It wouldn't wash off with water. You'd have to use soap and scrub it off."

"Like some glues?" Roy asked.

"Yeah... like glue." Suki smiled a little. "Except it would dry fast and not be sticky, and it would be safe for humans."

Roy smiled back and let out a light laugh. "Yeah... you wouldn't want everything sticking to you."

"Exactly... my grandmother thought of everything."

"Sounds like she may have thought too much." It was all beginning to make a little more sense to Roy.

"I guess." Suki picked up the flickering flashlight. A few quick shakes kept it bright for the time being. "My grandmother was the smartest person I've ever known, and her lab was my favorite place to be."

"How did you see her when you were living all over the world?"

"I'd spend summers with her, and we were together most holidays. While my parents slept, we created all kinds of things in her lab," Suki said, seeming to get lost in the past for a couple of seconds.

"So... you worked at night because of your skin

problem?"

"Maybe . . . I never really thought about it. It was just easier for both of us. Nothing could stop us from finding a solution—not the sun, my parents, or anyone else. And once we realized what we had actually created, the night became a much easier place to keep the secret."

Roy smirked. "I can understand that. The night is the perfect place to keep a secret."

"What about your brain, Roy Winklesteen? Is that a good place to keep a secret?" Suki asked, shining the light in his face.

"It's the only place for a secret that's better than the night." Roy pushed the flashlight away. "You have nothing to worry about."

Suki returned the flashlight to the floor between them. "We experimented with things like microscopic glass beads, titanium oxide, and mica powder. We were working on a combination that would block the rays and not be visible once it dried. I mean, she didn't want me to have to walk around looking all shiny or white."

"That's it," Roy interrupted. "That's what went wrong. It must have been whatever you added to make the stuff dry clear . . . right?" Roy cocked his head back and grinned proudly. "Instead of clear, it made things invisible."

"That's a good guess." Suki had a hint of surprise on her face. "That's what my grandmother thought. We worked on a lot of sprays with different combinations of materials. We were in the middle of testing when she got sick."

"Oh . . . she got sick?"

"Yeah." Suki's voice got lower and quieter. "So, on days she was feeling well enough, she taught me everything she knew and left me with all her stuff."

"Wow . . ." Roy said, "no wonder you're so smart."

Suki's long face tightened a little, and a slight smile crept in between her full cheeks. She took the flashlight and walked over to a metal filing cabinet in the corner of the shed. She pulled on a string-like necklace from under her shirt with a clump of keys dangling from it. "Hold the flashlight."

Roy took the light and pointed it at her hands. She thumbed through the keys and secured the smallest one between her fingers. "You're not seeing any of this . . . right?"

"Seeing what?" Roy gave her his most secretive look.

Suki unlocked the top drawer of the cabinet with the key and pulled out a brown leather book. "These are all my grandmother's notes. She wrote down everything we did together to make the spray and even things she did without me."

Roy shined the light on the book. It looked really important—like it should be somewhere other than an old filing cabinet in an old shed. Suki thumbed through the pages. As each white sheet revealed itself in the light, Roy caught glimpses of formulas, drawings, lists, dates, and notes.

"Right before she died, she made me promise that I would protect our secret and keep working on what we had started together. She told me that when I got old enough, I would have the wisdom to figure out whether or not the world should know about what we had invented." She took the flashlight from Roy and aimed it at his face again. "I hope she's right. And I hope I didn't make a mistake letting you see my lab."

"You have nothing to worry about," Roy said. "I get it now. Invisibility could be awesome in the hands of good people and terrifying in the hands of evil people. I can think of some people I would never want to have that power."

"Exactly," Suki said.

Roy reached out to the book and ran his pointer finger across an equation he found especially interesting and mumbled to himself. "Still, if it does make people invisible, then it's the most amazing spray ever."

Suki slammed the book closed on Roy's finger and placed it back in the cabinet. "It DOES make people invisible, and it's not just one spray—it's two."

"Okay . . . jeez . . . sorry."

One thing was for sure. Her secret was much better than his, and a lot of questions had been answered. But Roy was dying to know more—everything. "So, are the sprays in there?"

Suki walked to the shed door and slightly opened it. "I think you've seen enough for tonight."

"Wait . . ." Roy followed her. "Don't I get to see the actual spray?"

"Not tonight." Suki opened the door all the way. "I will get my lab set up tomorrow, and maybe I will show you then."

"Maybe?" Roy wasn't giving up now. He shut the shed door. "What do you mean maybe? I already know about it. What's the big deal in showing me how it works?"

"I'm still not sure I totally trust you." She gestured for him to leave. "You might try to steal it or something."

"If we are the only two people who know about it,

then wouldn't it be obvious I stole it?"

"Whatever. Not tonight . . . you need to leave. You've got school tomorrow."

Suki looked tired, so Roy decided to give her a break—for now.

She pushed him out the door and followed him to her front yard. "That's your bus stop over there . . . right?" Suki pointed to the corner across the street and to her right.

"Yeah . . . that's it."

"What time do you have to be there?"

"Seven-thirty."

"Ugh . . . so early?" Suki flashed him a smug look like she was glad it was him and not her that had to get up so early. "Eleven tomorrow night—okay?"

Roy nodded and ran across the street to his house.

CHAPTER 11

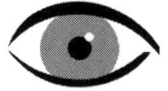

AWESOME!

The morning buzz on the bus was that Blob had been suspended from school for the entire week. The reason for his suspension was unclear, but that didn't stop the rumors from traveling from one kid to another at the speed of light.

"I heard he stole a test from a teacher and sold it to other kids," a seventh-grader said.

Another butted in and said, "No . . . no, he stole a teacher's purse and sold all the stuff inside."

The entire bus was humming with stories—all of them not true as far as Roy was concerned.

"Can you believe this stuff?" Nicholas said, turning to Roy. "You know they are just making stuff up."

Roy looked around at all the gossiping kids. "Yeah, no one knows that better than us," he replied. "Maybe he wasn't suspended at all. Maybe he's home recovering from the beating you gave him yesterday." Both boys laughed and tuned out all the nonsense.

Roy was relieved that he had the rest of the week to breathe easy and keep his math homework to himself. Also, things with Nicholas seemed to be back on track. That was the great thing about rumors—once a new one popped up, all the others seemed to lose their voice.

Roy knew that he was going to have to deal with Blob eventually. But for now, he could stop worrying about school and focus on what the nights had to offer. He was glad he had not given up on Suki. Sure, she was bossy and made jokes at his expense, but for everything he didn't like about her, there was one really big thing he did like.

After school, he hid out in his room and finished his homework early. Then he researched as much as he could about invisibility and other subjects Suki seemed to know so much about.

At exactly 10:59 p.m., Roy was already half-way to Suki's house. He walked around the big tree in her yard and whispered her name. He even looked in the tree and all around the front, but Suki was nowhere in sight. He tiptoed into her backyard. Roy grinned when he saw the light coming from the shed's small, curtained window.

Once at the door, he hesitated. Should he barge in? Perhaps not. Instead, he tapped on the rough, painted door with his knuckles. After a little commotion, Suki poked her head out.

"It's eleven already?" she asked.

"A little past," Roy confirmed.

"Sorry, I didn't meet you in the yard." She moved aside so Roy could enter. "I don't have a clock or a watch out here."

Roy shrugged. "That's okay. I knew where you would be. Should you have the light on?"

"Yeah . . . of course. My parents know I'm out here. I spent all day working on the place. They even got me some new stuff." Suki looked behind her and took in a deep breath of pride.

Roy looked around too. There were a couple of long tables that hugged the left corner walls, a desk chair at each table, some gray metal cabinets on the right wall, and a set of open shelves near the door. One table had a microscope with some small plastic bins next to it. The other table had a few glass containers, a couple of desk lamps, and some books. Dark, heavy drapes covered the window. All the dead bugs, spiderwebs, and dust were gone, and the place no longer smelled like it had the first time Roy saw it.

"Wow," Roy said. "It really looks like a lab. Like maybe something a mad scientist would have."

"Scientist—yes," Suki said while sitting down in front of the microscope. "Mad—no way. My head is screwed on extra tight."

"Aren't you afraid your parents will snoop?"

"They can snoop all they want," she said. "All the invisibility stuff is locked up. Besides, they probably wouldn't know what they were looking at even if they did see it."

Roy rolled a chair next to her. Invisibility—that was the word he wanted to hear. He was tired of waiting. "I think you have something to show me."

"So, you think you deserve to hold one of the greatest scientific breakthroughs human beings have ever created?" Suki walked over to the metal cabinet and pulled out the keys from under her shirt.

"Let's just put it this way," Roy started. "I already know too much for you to not show me the rest. Besides, all I've seen is invisible wrapping. How do I know it's not some trick—like magic? Isn't evidence always the most important factor in science?"

Roy leaned back in the chair and crossed his arms. For once, it was he who made a great argument, and

Suki was the one struggling to find her words. His body tingled with confidence—it felt like summer all over again.

Suki grimaced a little, but Roy knew better. She wanted to show him. Who wouldn't?

"Fine. I'll show you something simple so you can see how it works. Then, if I feel like I can still trust you—maybe—I will show you more." Suki opened up the bottom drawer and pulled out two clear plastic bottles. She returned to the table and sat back down. She slid them over in front of Roy.

Roy stared at the cheap-looking bottles. They reminded him of when he was seven and fascinated with the old west. For about a year, all he talked about was cowboys, campfires, and horses. He had begged his mom for a squirt gun, but Helen Winklesteen didn't like guns. So, on Halloween night, Roy had to settle for a generic spray bottle in his cowboy holster. He had forgotten all about the old west, and he was sure his face showed how much he didn't care to remember.

"You have to swear you won't tell anyone about what you see tonight," Suki said.

"You mean what I don't see."

"You know what I mean."

"C'mon, why would I tell?" Roy said. "Besides, you

know a really embarrassing secret of mine... remember?"

Still giving Roy a suspicious eye, Suki tore off a piece of paper from a yellow notepad next to the microscope. She crumpled it up until it was about the size of a golf ball.

She slid out of the chair and bent down toward the floor. She placed the ball of paper close to Roy's feet. Roy leaned over in the chair, resting his elbows on his thighs.

Suki tapped Roy's leg with her open palm. "Hand me the bottle with the blue squirt top."

Roy placed the bottle in her hand. Suki shook the bottle and gave the piece of paper two quick mists. She looked up at Roy, "We have to wait for this layer to dry."

She handed the bottle back to Roy. He shook the bottle and brought it up to his face. "So, what's in this stuff?"

"Silver mica powder and titanium oxide... plus a couple of other things." Suki looked up from the piece of paper. "That's all I can tell you."

"What does the spray do... exactly?" Roy asked. "I mean, why did your grandmother choose to use the silver... stuff and titanium ox—"

"Titanium oxide?" Suki interrupted. "My grandmother used them because they have protective and reflective qualities. But when she combined them with all the other stuff, they did more than that. She said that when all the materials are working together, the light reacts in a way nature never thought of doing."

"Okay," Roy said, trying hard to understand what Suki was explaining. "And that would be the invisibility part, right?"

"Yeah." Suki touched the wad of paper to check for moisture. "My grandmother said that we created a metamaterial that bent the light around objects instead of absorbing or reflecting it."

Invisibility: Roy wondered why nature hadn't thought of it. Or had it? Sure, there was camouflage, but that wasn't really invisibility, at least not the type Suki and her grandmother had created.

Then again, maybe there were invisible objects on Earth, and humans didn't know about them. But if there were, wouldn't humans have found them by now? Roy shook his head and blinked his eyes several times. He reminded himself to stop thinking so much and enjoy the moment. Besides, he understood the basic principle.

"So, it's like an invisible bubble of protection around you?" Roy asked. "Like the wrapper around the candy."

"I guess that's one way of putting it." Suki held out her hand. "Now, get the bottle with the clear squirt top."

Roy gripped the clear-top bottle.

"Shake it and give the piece of paper two good mists."

As he pulled the trigger, a nervous excitement tickled his arm. He couldn't believe what he was doing.

"Now, we wait." Suki stared at the paper.

Roy slid out of the chair and onto his knees. He didn't dare take his eyes off the wad of paper either.

"Brace yourself . . ." she said. "You're not going to believe what you are about to see."

Neither of the two said anything else. They waited and watched.

Roy's eyes got bigger and bigger as the piece of paper got fainter and fainter until it completely disappeared.

"Told you," Suki said. "It's pretty crazy and kind of hard to believe—which is why we need to keep it simple tonight."

"Whoa—that's awesome." He looked at the bottle still in his hand. "So, whatever is in this spray is reacting with whatever is in the other spray?"

"Exactly." Suki nodded. "All this spray was supposed to do was make the first spray waterproof and not shiny. But—"

"It makes things invisible." Roy felt around on the floor for the piece of paper. When he finally found it, he picked it up and put it in his other hand.

"I bet you're glad you told me your secret now," Suki said.

"For sure—hey, look." Roy pinched the paper between his fingers. "I can see the bottom."

"We didn't spray the bottom, so of course, you can see it."

"That explains why I could see the inside of the wrapper last night." Roy twisted his wrist so that the bottom came into full view. It looked like a small piece of paper crumpled up but still flat. "This is so weird," Roy said. His fingers appeared to be pinching air with a floating piece of yellow paper orbiting around his fingers every time he rotated his wrist. "You're right. You have to see it to understand it. Last night, my brain had a hard time making sense of what my eyes were seeing."

Suki reached for the paper. "Let me spray the rest of it."

She returned the paper to the floor with the visible side facing up. Then she gave it two quick mists.

"Why didn't the floor disappear?" Roy asked.

"A little bit of it did." Suki rubbed her hand on the rough concrete floor near the paper. "What you are seeing is what didn't get sprayed—which looks just like what did get sprayed."

"Huh?" All of this was blowing Roy's mind.

"You're seeing the concrete that was around the paper," Suki explained.

Roy squinted at the floor. "I guess I understand."

"That's what my grandmother and I were trying to do—understand," Suki said. "We were just starting to test different combinations to find out which materials were causing the invisibility. If we had figured that out, then we could have changed the spray to still keep me safe but not make me disappear."

"So that's what you are still trying to do—in your new lab? And your parents know everything except the invisibility part?"

"Yeah, it's not like I have the money to buy all this stuff," she said. "They just know that I am getting close to making it work."

"I guess you can say it works better than you want." Roy wished he had a lab or a workshop.

"Sure, the invisibility part is great, and it does protect me. But I don't want to be invisible . . . at least not most of the time." She chuckled.

"Still, if you had to make a mistake . . . this is the best one ever." Roy's eyes remained fixated on the piece of paper.

"Yeah, most scientists don't get that lucky when they make a mistake. It's been so much fun making things invisible that I haven't worked much on the visible part." Suki poked the bottle in Roy's hand. "You know what to do."

Roy shook the bottle and gave the paper two quick mists. Within a few seconds, what was left of the paper began to fade. "I still can't believe what I'm seeing."

"You mean what you're not seeing."

Roy looked at the girl he had once called "strange" in disbelief. He couldn't have been happier that she had moved in across the street. So what if she was a little annoying? Her secret more than made up for it. The past few days were almost as unbelievable as the spray itself, and he was certain his life was going to get a lot more interesting—thanks to the spray, of course.

It took every ounce of the maturity his parents told him he should have to stop himself from running around the room and doing cartwheels.

But he kept his cool.

"How close were you and your grandmother to figuring out the invisibility part?"

"Not far at all." Suki's smile disappeared from her face. "We were just beginning to test when my grandmother started feeling bad."

Sorrow filled the air. Roy started to feel guilty about being so excited and knew he had to say something. "I bet your grandmother is really proud you are going on with everything. I'm sure you'll eventually solve the problem."

"I hope my grandmother doesn't know I showed you the spray," Suki said, returning the bottles back to the file drawer and locking it. "She would say over and over again that no one could know about it."

"Thanks for trusting me," Roy said.

"Me too," Suki said.

"Maybe your grandmother wouldn't mind you showing one person. Don't scientists work in teams?" Roy studied Suki's face. "You and your grandmother worked together. Maybe she told you that so you would realize how important it was to keep things quiet and not to brag about it to all your friends."

"Maybe." Suki shrugged. "But that doesn't give you the right to tell anyone or tell me what to do. It's my experiment."

"I get it," he reassured her. Roy felt around on the floor until he found the piece of paper. "Can I keep this?"

"Okay," Suki said. "But don't show it to anyone."

"I'll try not to."

They both laughed.

Roy tucked the invisible clump of paper into his jeans pocket. "I'd better get going. You know—school and all."

"Yeah," Suki said. "Come by again tomorrow night. If you think that wad of paper in your pocket is hard to believe, wait until we make other stuff invisible."

"Oh, don't worry. I'll be here," Roy said as he opened the shed door.

"I don't worry," Suki said. "I'm not like you."

CHAPTER 12

OOPS.

Roy returned to his room. He scooped the paper ball out of his pocket and looked around for a secure place to put it. With his left hand, he grabbed a pencil cup from his desk and dumped the contents into the drawer.

He opened his right hand above the cup and let the wad of paper fall to the bottom. He swirled the cup around and listened to it hitting the sides. He still couldn't believe what he wasn't seeing.

After getting ready for bed, he crawled under the covers with the cup in his hand. He needed a better place to put it. His mom was always cleaning, and she was bound to unknowingly do something with it.

Roy reached far under his bed and pulled out his secret treasure box that he had made in Boy Scouts. He opened it and found the Invisoscript Bart had given him on their last day together.

He turned over the cup and let the paper fall into his hand. With the Invisoscript, he scribbled some temporary marks on the wad of paper.

That was better, Roy thought. Now he wouldn't have to worry about dropping and losing it for the next new minutes. Even with just his desk lamp on, he could see the lines from the pen floating around as he moved his hand.

According to Suki, the spray on the paper was somehow bending the light around the object so he couldn't see it. Wavelengths, reflection, refraction, UV light, metamaterials—Roy didn't really understand any of it. But that made what he wasn't seeing even more mesmerizing.

As the lines from the Invisoscript started to fade, he returned the pen to the box and placed the paper next to it. He took a moment to admire the contents. When he made the box a few years ago, he had never dreamed he would have a pen with evaporating ink and an invisible piece of paper.

He slid the box back under his bed and tried to get some sleep. It was hard to turn his mind off, knowing what he had seen and what he still might see—or not see—or whatever—anyway, it was all amazing.

The next day at school, Roy's mind continued to beg for an opportunity to be heard. Just like the first time he saw Bart leap off his roof with a pair of wings strapped to his arms, he struggled not to tell anyone about his latest secret. He would undoubtedly be the most popular kid in school if everyone knew what he was doing at night. No one would ever think he was a loser again—especially his best friend.

Yet, he didn't dare open his mouth. Bart's and Suki's trust mattered much more to him than anything his classmates could offer. He reminded himself that the only reason he had any awesome secrets was because of his trustworthiness.

Roy kept quiet at school, and Blob's absence kept the day uneventful.

When Roy reached Suki's lab, he didn't bother knocking. Suki twirled around in her chair as he entered. "Lock the door," she said.

Roy looked at the door. He didn't know it locked.

"The hook and loop—at the top."

Roy found the hook and swung the end into the metal loop. He took a deep breath and tried to keep his enthusiasm in check.

He blinked his eyes a few times and took two steps

toward Suki. "What are those?" he asked, keeping a cautious distance.

"These are my test subjects," Suki said, holding out her hand and offering one to Roy.

Roy looked at the wrinkly, pink, wiggling creature in her hand and then looked at the clear container holding at least five more of the little critters.

"Go ahead, take her," Suki said. "If you're going to hang out in my lab, you're going to have to make friends with these little buggers."

Roy crept closer to Suki's hand. He wasn't sure what to do. He had never held a mouse before—especially one without hair.

"Here," she insisted. "She won't bite—she's really friendly. I named her Uno—you know, like number one—only in Spanish."

"Why is it bald?" Roy asked, taking a few steps closer.

"It's the type of mouse—they're hairless. It's good for testing UV protection," Suki explained. "I use the ones with hair too." Suki pulled another rectangular plastic container from back behind the other.

Roy wrapped his hands around the mouse. It felt oddly smooth, tickly, and surprisingly warm. It was taking every bit of strength he had not to jerk his hands back and let the sort-of-ugly-looking-but-in-a-cute-way creature fall to the ground.

Suki turned back toward the desk. "You hold her while I finish up this new spray for testing. It'll only take a minute."

While Suki concentrated on her formula, Roy peeped between the gaps of his fingers. He couldn't believe he was actually holding a mouse—especially a bald one. Man, would he love to put one of these in Melonie's bed.

His parents would never buy him one mouse, much less a dozen. They wouldn't even get a fish. His mom wanted nothing to do with animals. It wasn't that she didn't like them. She just didn't think that animals and humans were meant to live together, and everyone else in the family went along with it. But ever since he'd met Shirley, Bart's dog, Roy had thought it would be cool to have a furry friend. They were good companions, and it would be nice to have some company at night. Plus, he could do anything in front of a dog—it's not like it would ever tell anyone.

Roy opened his hands a little wider. He stared into the mouse's tiny eyes. It calmed down and stared back. It was no big deal—holding a mouse, he reassured himself. It was actually kind of nice. They weren't the mischievous, dirty little squatters so many people made them out to be. Roy chuckled. His mom would have a fit if she knew so many mice lived across the street.

"Okay, hand her over." Suki stretched her arm out and wiggled her fingers.

Roy gave the mouse a quick stroke on the head. "See ya later, lil' bit."

"No, you shouldn't see her later." Suki took the mouse. "This formula should still make her disappear. I'm testing for other things right now."

"Oh . . . well, I guess the plan is to not see you later," Roy said.

Suki placed the mouse in a rectangular-shaped wire box. It looked like a miniature dog or cat cage. "I administer the spray in this. She'll move around enough to get completely covered without being able to squirm away."

She dipped a Q-tip into a jug of Vaseline near the mouse containers. "I put a dab of this on her closed eyes and mouth. We don't want her swallowing the spray or getting it in her eyes."

Roy watched in awe as Suki's steady hand applied the gooey substance. The mouse froze on the wire bottom, as though it knew she was doing it a favor.

She got the bottle of formula, shook it, and looked at

Roy. "Here it goes." Suki gave the mouse two quick blasts from the top, bottom, and sides.

The mouse circled the cage and reached for the top a few times.

"It looks scared," Roy said. "Are you sure this stuff isn't going to hurt her?"

"Like I said, my grandmother made sure it was safe." Suki kept her eye on the mouse, which seemed to calm down. "Remember, she was a scientist, and I'm her granddaughter. She wasn't about to make anything that would hurt me."

"Then why use a mouse to test the stuff?" Roy asked. "Why not use yourself?"

"Three reasons," Suki said, putting the wire box on the table. "One, they are small and don't require nearly as much spray. Two, their skin reacts the same way as human skin does to UV rays, and three, I can't be exposed to UV rays, remember? What happens if the spray doesn't work?"

"But your skin is different, isn't it?" Roy asked.

"Yeah, but the point is to make a coating that won't let any UV rays in at all and that will stay on unless washed off or scraped off. Plus, scientists use mice for all types of experimentation." Suki focused her attention back on the mouse and administered the second spray. "It just made sense to her—and me."

"If it makes sense to you, then it makes sense to me." Roy watched the mouse as Suki finished writing her notes. "Oh my gosh . . ." Roy leaned in over the cage. "It's almost completely gone."

"Yep, this seems like it will be a good batch." She lifted the wire box up and studied it from all sides. "And I got good coverage."

She opened the top of the cage and scooped out the mouse. "You're not going to believe this." Suki cradled the almost completely invisible mouse in her hands and wiped off the excess Vaseline. "The spray doesn't work on wet surfaces."

Suki opened up her hands and brought them close to Roy's face.

"That's amazing," he said. Her hands looked empty except for the two tiny floating eyes and slit of a mouth moving around going in and out of sight. It was the most bizarre thing he had ever seen.

"You should see her eat a piece of cheese—it's freaky."

"Do you have any cheese?"

"You can feed her in a bit." Suki closed her hands around the mouse and moved over to the next table, where a plastic box sat with a black cloth stuffed inside it and a desk lamp cantilevering over it. "Right now, I need to get her under the UV light."

"Can I hold her?" Roy asked.

"Alright, I have to set a few things up anyway." She opened her hands and tilted Uno into Roy's hands. "Don't let her get away. It's easier than you think."

"I won't." Roy wrapped his hands around the squirming creature. Suki got busy working on the light.

Roy opened his hands like a clamshell. Two beady, floating, black eyes stared at him. He opened his hands a little wider and then a little more and then a little too much.

Roy felt a lot of scratching. Then the tiny eyes and mouth poked out of his hands and fell to the ground. "OH . . . NO."

Suki twisted around. "What happened?"

Roy held up his empty hands.

"Where's the mouse?"

"I-it got free."

"Well, don't just stand there." Suki fell to her hands and knees and started crawling around on the floor. "Look for her, you big dummy."

Roy got down on the ground next to her and began patting the floor.

Suki crawled around and centered in on the scurrying in the corner near the filing cabinet. "I hear her. She's somewhere over here. Look for the eyes."

Roy crawled over next to her. "Yeah..." he said. "I think it's behind the cabinet. I'll get that empty bin over there so we can trap her."

"Hurry, and grab the flashlight."

Roy retrieved the bin and fumbled around for the flashlight.

"Give me the bin," Suki commanded.

Roy shook the flashlight until it flickered on and then kneeled down to help Suki push the bin toward the corner of the shed.

"Got her." She stood up and placed the bin on the table. "There," she said. "Disaster averted." She swung around and gave Roy a disappointed scowl. "If you're going to help, you need to be more careful." She turned her back to Roy.

"Sorry... this is all so new for me."

"Fine, I guess I understand, but it can't happen again," Suki said, looking up at him. "It wouldn't be good to have a set of floating mouse eyes running around the neighborhood."

Roy looked in the bin. Two black dots nervously floated around close to the edge. Sometimes, the eyes would completely disappear when the mouse was looking away. The whole situation made Roy feel a little mischievous. "But it could be kind of funny."

Suki sighed. "See? That's exactly what my grandmother was talking about. It's so easy to use this stuff the wrong way."

Roy felt bad for being so clumsy. And even though it would have been hilarious to watch his sister run from a set of floating mouse eyes, he completely understood that it wasn't the best use of the spray.

So, he had to ask, "What's the right way?"

Suki paused for a minute. "Huh, I have never thought about it. I guess it would be great for spying on bad people and catching them doing bad things—but then it would be so easy to spy that it really wouldn't be fair to call yourself a spy."

"True... but even someone who's not a spy could use it to fight evil. That would be good... right?" Roy asked.

"It would, except my grandmother seemed to think that invisibility might actually have the power to turn someone good into someone evil." Suki reached into the bin and tried to grab the invisible mouse. "You know—having all that power can make someone crazy."

"I guess... when you think about it, being invisible

is about being able to get away with doing things and not getting caught," Roy said. "And who doesn't want to get caught doing something good?"

"Yeah, that's the whole idea," Suki said. "See, my grandmother knew what she was talking about."

CHAPTER 13

HA . . . HA, VERY FUNNY.

Suki and Roy sat at the table in silence as they both watched the two black dots dart around the bin. They could hear the mouse scratching on the sides, as though trying to climb its way out.

"Wanna have some fun?" Suki asked, holding the bottles of spray.

"Why do you think I'm here?"

"See that mini fridge over there?" Suki said, waving the spray bottle toward the metal files.

Roy followed Suki's eyes. He hadn't noticed it before. "Yeah."

"Get the cheese out of it."

Roy grinned and took the cheese from the square black cube.

"Break a piece off and give it to her."

Roy broke off a piece of cheese and dropped it right in the center of the bin. The eyes slightly teetered their way from the side and stopped near the yellow-orange chunk. The piece wobbled a little before rising off the bottom.

"I see its teeth. And there's its tongue." Roy bent down for a closer look. "This is so bizarre. It's a floating mouth with floating eyes—eating cheese."

Suki picked out a hairy mouse from the group in the other bin and placed it next to the floating piece of cheese. "It freaks them out."

Roy threw his head back in laughter. "This is so crazy. Look—the hairy mouse doesn't know what to do. You can tell it wants the cheese so bad, but it's not going anywhere near those scary eyes. I wonder what it's thinking."

Roy watched the hairy mouse hug the corner of the bin. It looked so scared and helpless. He stopped laughing and bent down closer to the frightened creature. He felt bad for it. Suki was doing to the visible mouse what Roy had envisioned doing to Melonie. He wondered why Suki thought it was okay to be mean to a mouse but not to a human. What was the difference? Roy wondered.

"I'm going to put it back. It seems kind of cruel to

scare it like that." He gave the hairy mouse a couple of reassuring pets on its back and returned it to its friends.

"Oh... it'll be fine. I do it all the time." Suki retrieved the two spray bottles from the night before and held them up for Roy to see. "Now it's time for me to really freak you out." She aimed the bottle with the blue top right at her arm and began spraying.

"Wait," Roy said. "I thought you were only supposed to spray the mice?"

"No, only the new formulas are tested on the mice. These formulas have already been tested, and they're safe for me."

Suki waited a few minutes and then sprayed her hand with the second bottle.

They both locked their eyes on her hand.

"No... way," Roy whispered. "This has gotta be a dream."

"Nope, it's real." Suki moved her arm closer to Roy's face. "Is this enough evidence for you?"

Roy couldn't stop staring. Right in front of him was Suki's arm—with no hand. It didn't look gross like it had been cut off. Instead, it just wasn't there—like it had been erased.

Suki pointed to her wrist. "See, if you don't get

complete coverage, then the electromagnetic waves get scattered, and our eyes see some of the object."

"Your wrist looks like a ghost's wrist. Man . . . this is amazing." Roy poked Suki's invisible hand. "I can think of a million things I'd like to do with those spray bottles."

"I know," Suki said. "I have a hard time not spraying everything—just to see what happens."

"Can I borrow some?" Roy asked. "My mom has been getting on to me about cleaning my room, and this spray would make it so easy."

Suki started laughing. "Yeah, but the mess would still be there. You'd just be tripping over all of it. And you wouldn't be able to find anything."

"True . . . maybe I could spray my sister instead. It would be nice to make her disappear—at least sometimes," Roy said. "But I would still be able to hear her, so I guess it would be a waste of spray."

"Here." Suki handed the first bottle to Roy. "Give it a try."

Roy took the bottle. Holding it made him a little nervous. He wasn't sure what to do with it. There were so many options.

"Well . . . don't just stand there. Spray something," Suki said, looking around the lab.

He peeled off his tennis shoe with his other foot and flung it to the middle of the floor. "Let's see what it does to a tennis shoe." Roy kneeled down and gave the top and sides of the shoe a good dousing.

"Huh . . . I've never sprayed a shoe," Suki said. "This should be interesting."

"It'll probably take a little while to dry . . . right?" Roy asked.

"Yeah, let's see how the mouse is doing."

They returned to the bin and looked inside. The cheese chunk was gone, and the eyes were hovering in a corner.

"I need to test this formula." Suki struggled to drape the thick black cloth over the lamp, so it fully covered the bin. "Having an invisible hand is making me clumsy." She felt around with her visible hand until she was able to switch the lamp on. "Let me set this timer, and then we can have some more fun."

Roy felt his shoe. "It's dry, so I guess I should spray it with the other one, right?"

"Sounds good to me."

Roy smothered his shoe with the second spray. He wanted to spray his hand so bad, but he was still a little scared. "How do you know your hand won't stay that way?"

"Oh, I know it won't." Suki ran her long fingernail across the top of her invisible hand. "See, it's like a covering. You can scrape it off with something rough or sharp—especially on things like skin or plastic or metal. Clothes—that's a different story. They have to be washed to completely reappear." Suki moved her finger away and revealed a translucent line of pinkish-brown skin.

"Whoa." Roy touched the floating line. "This all seems like a dream."

"I know," Suki said, continuing to scrape more dried spray off her hand.

Roy looked back toward the floor.

"Oh . . . my SHOE."

"Well . . . what did you think was going to happen, brainiac?" Suki said.

Roy dropped to his knees and began feeling around on the floor with his hands. "There it is." He flipped the shoe over to reveal the unsprayed bottom. "I totally forgot. These are my new school shoes. I can't take them home like this."

Roy slipped the shoe back on and began scraping the side with his bitten fingernail. "It's not working."

"I told you it doesn't work the same on everything," Suki said. "It's probably because the shoe is fabric. See?

Look at your other one."

Roy scraped harder. "What am I gonna do?"

"Put it in the washing machine," Suki said.

"I don't know how to use a washing machine," Roy said. "Besides, even if I did, my mom would be suspicious about why I was using it."

"It's no big deal," Suki said. "The next time you hear the washing machine going, just throw it in there. And when your mom pulls everything out, she'll think it got mixed up with your dirty clothes."

Roy smiled. "Yeah... that should work. Except what about the bottom? It might be a while until I can get it in the wash. My mom might see it if I leave it in my room. She's always cleaning up, and she doesn't miss anything."

Roy sat down on his bottom and held up his invisible foot with the bottom facing Suki. "This will completely freak her out."

Suki got the spray bottles. "You worry too much." She gave the bottom of the shoe several quick blasts of spray. "It needs a heavy coating since you'll be walking on it. It's not fabric like the top and won't soak it in."

Roy tilted the sprayed bottom toward his face. "I guess I should be more careful about what I spray."

"You think?"

"I should let it dry before I step on it." He took his shoe off with the fading bottom face up. "My turn, again," he said, grabbing the spray bottle out of Suki's hand.

"Hey . . . I'm not sure I should trust you. Look what you did to your shoe," Suki said, putting her hand on the bottle. "All this stuff in here is mine. I don't want you spraying just anything."

Roy looked at Suki's sprayed hand. She had managed to scrape off several patches. It looked weird and cool at the same time. "Fine . . . I'll spray myself."

"Go for it," Suki said, letting go of the bottle.

Roy held his arm out over the empty shed floor. Suki backed away. "Here it goes."

Roy gave his hand and lower part of his arm several sprays. He rotated everything around to ensure complete coverage. After a few minutes, he followed up with the second spray. A big grin filled his face as he anticipated the outcome.

Suki gasped and brought her hands to her mouth. "OH NO . . . I completely forgot."

Roy's eyes got really big. "What . . . what do you mean you forgot something? Tell me."

"It doesn't work the same on boys," Suki said.

"What does that mean?" Roy's voice sounded a little

panicked. "How would you even know that? When have you tested this stuff on a boy?"

"The mice... we used to have boys and girls, but every time we sprayed the boy mice, we couldn't reverse the invisibility by washing them off." Suki looked down at Roy's almost invisible hand and lower arm. "Nothing seemed to work. My grandmother tried everything. They became invisible... forever." Suki looked toward the two bins of mice. "See? Those are all girls." She walked over to the window and pulled the curtain back. "Somewhere out there is an invisible boy mouse just running around, dying to be seen."

Roy looked at his hand and lower arm. He spit on his arm several times and began scraping and rubbing it. "Why didn't you say something? Who forgets something so important like that?"

Suki turned away from the window. "It looks cool. Think of how popular you will be. You'll probably make the national news."

Then she held her belly and began laughing.

Roy stopped rubbing his arm and looked at her. His panic turned to anger. "Ha... ha. You think you're so funny. Well... you're not... you're mean."

She stopped laughing. "Oh... c'mon. I'm just having some fun. I mean... look what we're doing.

How can we not make it funny?"

Roy bent down and began feeling for his tennis shoe. "You know . . . things aren't fun or funny when you're the only one in the room laughing at what you did."

Roy felt his shoe and slid it on his foot. "I'm sick of you making me look stupid." He stood up and looked Suki right in the eyes. "I'm a lot of things, but I'm definitely not stupid."

Suki reached for his invisible arm. "Ok . . . you're right. I thought you would think it was funny, especially after all that talk about scaring Melonie and making her disappear."

Roy glared at her and opened the shed door. "That's the problem. You don't know what is funny."

"Well, since you're so smart, why don't you teach me?" Suki pulled him toward her. "I really mean that. I know you're smart. Maybe that's why I feel comfortable giving you a hard time."

Roy's angry face relaxed a little. "I mean . . . it's easy to be funny by making fun of someone or tricking them," Roy explained. "It takes a lot more smarts to be funny without someone else having to pay for it."

Suki wiped the smirk off her face. "Okay. That makes sense. From now on, I'll try to make stuff, not people, funny."

Roy pulled his arm away and stepped outside into the brisk fall air. "I guess it was a little funny. I should've known being a boy wouldn't make a difference. Still, I need to go—you know—school and all."

"Same time tomorrow?" Suki asked.

Roy nodded.

"Bring some stuff you want to make disssaaaaappearrrr," she said, waving her hands like a magician.

"Oh . . . I will." Roy turned around and rushed off between the houses.

CHAPTER 14

GUESS WHO?

Roy made it to the fire escape but found it almost impossible to climb with an invisible hand. So, he closed his eyes and felt his way up.

Once in his room, he removed his invisible shoe and put it on his desk. He flicked on his lamp and aimed it at the spot where he knew his shoe was sitting. Where do you hide something invisible? he wondered. Roy looked around his room. Then he slid under his bed and stuffed his shoe behind his box of secret treasures. His mom would never stumble upon it there. And if she asked why he was wearing his old shoes, he was confident he would think of something clever.

He threw the other shoe way back in his closet and snuck down the hall toward the bathroom.

"Roy?" his dad whispered from his parents' bedroom

door. "Is that you?"

Roy jerked his arm behind him and looked at his dad. "Yeah . . . I have to use the bathroom."

"Why are you still in your clothes?"

Roy remained calm. "I fell asleep in them . . . doing my homework."

"Hurry up and get back to bed. You're going to wake up Melonie," his dad said, retreating back into the bedroom and partially closing the door.

Roy locked the bathroom door behind him and started scrubbing his arm and hand with warm water and soap. The membrane felt like gritty, peeling skin. He breathed a sigh of relief when all his body parts were equally visible.

Once tucked in bed, Roy thought about Suki, her invisible spray, and their budding friendship. He was still a little angry at her for making a fool of him—even though he had to admit that he was sort of an easy target.

Why was he so stupid around her? Why was he so stupid around most girls? Even Melonie could make him look small and stupid, and she was only seven.

Roy shook his head and rubbed his eyes. He felt stupid for wasting precious sleep time thinking about why he felt stupid, so he closed his eyes and thought of all the things he was going to bring to Suki's lab to make invisible.

That made him happy, and he fell asleep in no time.

The morning arrived in a flash, and before Roy had a chance to fully wake up, he was already on his way to school with Nicholas by his side.

They were deep into a discussion about when they were going to see the new Spider-Man movie when the bus door opened at Blob's stop. Neither boy seemed to care and kept right on talking. After all, Blob was still suspended—right?

Wrong.

No one, especially Roy, expected to hear the familiar taunting voice and heavy footsteps *plomp* up the bus stairs. Blob was back and looked madder than ever. Even his chest hairs seemed to be staring everyone down.

Roy and Nicholas watched Blob and Rob make their way down the aisle. They knew what was going to happen. Everyone did.

"Move it," Blob said, gesturing to the kids behind Roy and Nicholas. Some shuffling occurred, and then Roy felt the familiar sting on the back of his head. "Hand it over, Tinkleweenie. I haven't got all day."

Rob laughed and said, "Yeah . . . you have make-up

work to copy."

Nicholas looked at Roy. Roy looked straight ahead.

"Hey, doofus, you deaf or something?" Blob said, shoving his arm between Roy and Nicholas. He tapped Roy on the cheek with the back of his hand. "Give it here."

Nicholas grabbed Blob's arm and pushed it back. "Leave him alone," he said. "You're the doofus—copying math from a sixth-grader."

"What'd you say?" Blob pushed Nicholas's hand away and gripped his collar. "It's gonna be so much fun tearing you to shreds."

Enough of this, Roy thought. It was supposed to be HIS problem, not Nicholas's. No one was going to get beaten up over some stupid homework that only took Roy minutes to do, and the teacher only spent a few seconds checking.

Roy bent down and got his notebook out of his bag. "Leave him alone, and I'll give it to you," Roy said, securing the notebook in his lap.

"You threatening me . . . Tinkleweenie?" Blob let go of Nicholas's collar. "Afraid I'm gonna give your girlfriend a black eye?"

"Do you want it or not?" Roy asked while looking straight at Nicholas.

Blob stood halfway up, reached down, and snatched the notebook from Roy's lap. He held it high in the air out of both boys' reach. "I don't do deals. I get your homework, and I get to do whatever I want to your girlfriend over here." Blob gave Nicholas a death stare and sat back down.

Roy and Nicholas sat in complete silence for the rest of the bus ride.

The bus squeaked to a jerking stop in front of the school, and everyone immediately poured into the aisle. Blob didn't budge. Instead, he kept writing. "C'mon," Rob said, "give it back to the little loser in class—it's not like he's gonna need it."

Blob waved the notebook between the two boys. "Maybe you'll see it again, maybe you won't," Blob said, getting up from his seat and following Rob off the bus. He gave a quick glance back at Nicholas. "I'm not done with you."

The driver stood up and faced Blob. "Get off my bus," he said.

"Let's go," Rob said, grabbing Blob by the sleeve.

"You heard your friend . . . go . . . now," the driver said, pointing to the door. Then he looked back at Nicholas and Roy. "C'mon . . . boys . . . you too . . . let's move it."

Nicholas let out a huff and rushed off the bus. Roy followed close behind, but they got separated in a large group of kids standing in front of the sixth-grade wing. By the time Roy entered the hallway, Nicholas was already at his locker.

Roy needed to talk to his friend. Was he angry at Blob, or was he angry at him? Or was he angry at both of them?

He zigzagged around the small groups of kids lingering in the hall. He was almost to his best friend when Nicholas slammed his locker door and disappeared into the classroom.

That's when Roy knew. Nicholas was angry—at him. Roy hurried to his locker and scrambled to get his stuff together for first period. Right as he closed his locker, he heard a whisper in his ear.

Roy spun around, thinking it was Nicholas. But he saw no one near him. Roy looked around at all the kids chattering nearby. He must be hearing things. He shook it off and headed to class.

Then he heard it again, this time louder. "Hey, Roy Winklesteen, guess who?"

Roy turned toward the voice. No one was there. He twirled completely around.

"What, are you deaf?" the voice said, much louder.

Roy stopped breathing. A flush of terror covered his body. "Suki, is that you?"

CHAPTER 15

FFFFRRRRRRRRRT.

Roy froze in front of his locker.

"Of course, it's me," Suki said. "How many invisible people do you know?"

Roy looked around to see if anyone was watching him. Like always, no one seemed to be paying him any attention. He reopened his locker and faced the inside. "How'd you get here?" he asked. "Are you crazy?"

Suki giggled. "It was easy. I hopped on the bus right after you. What? You didn't see me?"

Roy was starting to freak out. "But... where did you sit? How'd you stay out of everyone's way?"

"Oh, that was no problem. I stood all the way in the back at the end of the aisle. One boy bumped into me, but he couldn't see me, so he blew me off."

Roy looked around again. He knew the first bell would be ringing soon, but he had to know more.

"Follow me."

Roy walked down the hall past his homeroom door. He slipped into an alcove with a couple of doors. When no one was looking, he turned the knob on the door labeled "storage." To his surprise, it was unlocked.

"Get in here," he said, not really sure where to look.

Roy could hear Suki follow him inside. He shut the door. It was totally dark. Roy felt for a light switch and flipped it on.

"What did you do that for?" Suki asked. "It's not like you can see me. And I already know what you look like."

"I just want it on . . . okay?" Roy was breathing so hard that he felt like he might pass out. "I can't believe you're here . . . at my school. What if the spray doesn't work? What if someone catches you? What if—"

"I've got all my protective gear on. See? I've even got my gloves on." Roy looked down and saw Suki's hand appear as she removed the glove. "I'm fine. I sprayed all my clothes . . . even my hat and hood. Nothing can get to me, and there's no way anyone can see me."

"Well . . . someone could hear you or feel you. I don't know . . . it's so crazy for you to be here."

"Relax. I already said that a boy bumped into me. All he did was look around, and when he didn't see anything, he kept right on going. People don't—"

Roy gasped. "Your shoe. I can see the end of your shoe." He pointed to the white blotch of leather floating slightly above the dark tiled floor. "Some of the spray must have scraped off."

"Stop worrying. I brought the bottles with me." Roy could hear Suki rummaging around. He heard a zipper, and then the contents to a small satchel were revealed. Roy didn't see the bottle but rather a few snacks and a pad of paper and some pens. "I sprayed the bottles just in case I want to carry them out in the open."

"I guess that was good thinking." Roy was feeling a little less dizzy.

"I bet a little of the second spray ought to do it," Suki said.

Roy could hear the spray as Suki touched up her shoe. "Still, you gotta get out of here. It's too risky."

"Relax. Don't be such a chicken—like you were with that big guy on the bus. You should have never bargained with him. People like him don't do bargains—that's their whole strategy." Suki returned the bottle and zipped up her bag. "See? The patch is almost gone. So, what class do we go to first?"

"NO WAY. You can't follow me around all day. Please go home."

"My ride doesn't get here until this afternoon. You know . . . it's called a bus. So, you're stuck with me."

Rrrriiiinnnnggg.

"Oops, you're late," Suki said. "We'd better get going." The light switched off, and the door opened. "Which way?"

Roy let out a little whimper and stepped out of the closet. Suki was right. He was late. As he walked to his homeroom class, his cheeks felt like two sirens yelling at everyone to get out of the way—disaster coming through.

Roy entered the open doorway. Everyone looked right at him. "Roy, take a seat please," Mrs. Scarsdale said, sounding a little miffed. "Next time you're late, I'll have to send you to the office to get a note."

Roy rushed to his seat next to Nicholas. Mrs. Scarsdale immediately picked back up on the class discussion about the book *The Giver*. Roy looked over at Nicholas. He was either really into the discussion or going out of his way to ignore his best friend.

And if that wasn't bad enough, Roy had a much bigger issue eating away at his brain: Suki.

He looked around the room. Where was she? Why was she doing this to him? How was he ever going to be able to concentrate in school when he knew Suki was watching his every move? Roy looked behind him. He knew she was probably right there; he just couldn't see her.

"Roy . . . Roy . . ." Mrs. Scarsdale said. "Roy, please pay attention. I asked you a question."

"I-I . . . what?" Roy responded. "I'm sorry. What was the question?"

Everyone stared at him.

"Please get with the discussion. There's nothing to see behind you," Mrs. Scarsdale snarled. "Nicholas," she continued, "can you help your friend out?"

Nicholas looked at Roy and then proceeded to answer the question. Roy sighed and looked down at his book. Great, he thought. Now Nicholas had to help him with schoolwork too. Could this day, which had barely started, get any worse?

Roy made it through English and his other morning class in the sixth-grade wing. Suki would whisper in his ear every once in a while, but she did a good job of going undetected.

It wasn't until he had to go to the eighth-grade wing that Roy began feeling queasy again. He was at his locker gathering up his math supplies when he remembered Blob still had his notebook.

"Where to next?" he heard Suki whisper in his right

ear. Roy tilted his math book in her direction and pointed to the word "Algebra."

"Well, this should be interesting," Suki whispered. "I wonder if you'll get your notebook back from that big guy."

Roy slammed his locker door. He could tell Suki was right beside him the entire walk to the eighth-grade wing. As he entered the hall, he felt a tug on his left arm. Roy turned. There stood Blob. He slapped the notebook right into Roy's chest. "You need to write neater. I can barely make out your scribble."

Suki whispered in Roy's ear, "He needs to be taught a lesson."

Roy looked in the direction of Suki's voice. "Stay out of it," he muttered without moving his lips. "You'll just make things worse."

"Yeah . . . well . . . we'll see about that."

Roy took his seat in the class. He tried to determine where Suki had settled in, but all the shuffling about and talking muffled her footsteps.

Mrs. Crowley shut the door and reminded everyone it was test day. Most of the kids let out a few moans and groans, but not Roy. He was ready to get lost in a world of numbers for an hour.

Once the test was in front of him, he turned his

attention to the problems on the paper and forgot about the ones in his life. By the third question, Roy had settled into a good rhythm until, out of nowhere, the loudest, juiciest sound filled the empty air.

Ppppppppfffffffftttttppppppiiiiishhhhhh.

Roy, along with the rest of the class, turned toward the sound, which came from the back row of desks that only one student occupied—Blob. Mrs. Crowley made him sit there for obvious reasons.

Snickers and giggles filled the room. Even Mrs. Crowley had to hide her grin.

Blob looked confused and flushed. "It wasn't me. I swear," he said. Everyone kept staring at him. "C'mon... I didn't do it."

"Alright, class, back to work," Mrs. Crowley said, clapping her hands and directing everyone's attention back to the front of the room. "It doesn't matter who did it. You have a test to complete, so get busy—only 37 minutes left."

The snickers and comments subsided, and everyone resumed their problem-solving—except Roy. He looked in Blob's direction a little longer. He let a big smile fill his face. Suddenly, Suki was the most awesome kid Roy had ever known. And she was right. Blob needed to be taught a lesson.

Pppppppfffffffffft. Fffffrrrrrrrrrrt.

The class looked back at Blob again. This time, the laughter and comments were louder. Mrs. Crowley walked back to Blob, bent down close to his ear, and whispered, "Do you need to be excused?"

"I-I didn't do it." Blob threw his pencil on his desk and looked behind him. "I don't know who's doing it, but it's not me."

"Yeah, right," one boy said. "It had to be you."

"Maybe it was a gassy ghost, Mrs. Crowley," another kid said. A burst of raucous laughter broke out.

"Alright . . . alright . . . that's enough. Get busy." Mrs. Crowley was almost back to her desk when it happened again.

Frrrrrrtpppppppiiiishhhhhh.

Mrs. Crowley looked at Blob and pointed to the door. "I think you need to be excused. You can finish the test later."

"I swear. It wasn't ME. I'm not the one doing it." Blob tensed up so much that Roy could see his shirt become tighter around his upper arms. He looked about two seconds away from spontaneously combusting. "It's coming from behind me."

"Yeah . . . it was your butt," someone said from the front of the class. "That's behind you."

Laughter, once again, filled the air. It was so loud that Roy was sure the principal would be alerted.

"Class, that's enough." Mrs. Crowley held out her arms as though she was trying to push down the noise. "Get back to work. And you . . ." She gestured to Blob. "Come with me."

Blob growled and scooched out of his seat. "I didn't do it."

"You can spend the rest of my class time with the school nurse." Mrs. Crowley wrote a quick note and handed it to Blob. "She can figure out what to do with you."

Blob turned and looked back at everyone in the class. "I didn't do it."

Mrs. Crowley shut the door and returned to her desk. She stared the class down until she could see the top of everyone's heads and hear nothing but the hum of the lights.

Roy looked back at where he thought Suki must have been sitting. He smiled the biggest he could ever remember. He was sure she was looking back—smiling as well.

CHAPTER 16

DON'T WORRY.

After math, Roy met up with the rest of the sixth-graders in the cafeteria. He assumed Suki was following him, but he couldn't be sure. He could tell Nicholas was still frustrated over what had happened on the bus, so Roy immediately provided him with a detailed account of what went down in Mrs. Crowley's class.

"Right in the middle of a test?" Nicholas asked, with gleeful eyes.

"Yep," Roy replied. "Three times, and they were long and squishy sounding."

"Maybe he has some stomach disease that will keep him out of school for the rest of the year." Nicholas sounded hopeful. "Maybe he'll be homeschooled."

"Yeah . . . maybe," Roy said, knowing that Blob was

still a problem. But if it put a smile on his friend's face, Roy was happy to agree.

The morning may have been stressful, but the rest of the day went great. Nicholas was happy. Blob got a taste of his own medicine, and Suki got to go to school and pull off one of the best pranks Roy had ever seen—or not seen.

The only problem was that Roy had not heard a peep out of Suki since math class. He tried whispering to her whenever possible, but she didn't respond.

The bus ride home was quiet as well. Blob sat in the back and never looked in Roy's or Nicholas's direction. Like most people, mornings seemed to make him extra grumpy.

As Roy got off the bus, he hung around at the corner, hoping to hear from Suki. "Miss me?" he heard her whisper in his ear.

"What happened to you?" Roy said, relieved to hear from her.

"Tell ya later." He could tell Suki was walking to her house. "I have to get home. See you tonight."

"Okay . . . tonight. See ya," Roy mumbled while looking around to see if anyone cared that he was talking to air.

"Hey, Roy." He turned toward Suki's voice.

"*Pfffffffttttffffffishhhhh*. Sound familiar?"

Roy let out a laugh and jogged home. The rest of the evening was no different than any other school night at the Winklesteen house, and Roy made it to Suki's at the regular time.

"So," Suki said, holding one of the hairy mice. "Did I surprise you today?"

"More like gave me a heart attack," Roy said, giving the mouse a pet on the head. "What you did to Blob today was awesome."

"Blob?"

"Well, that's what I call him—to myself—except I guess now you know."

"I like it." Suki smiled. "It fits him. He's kind of like a big, thoughtless ball of nothing that gets in the way without thinking about how he is hurting people."

"His friend's name is Rob."

"The Blob and Rob comedy hour." Suki looked up at the ceiling and put her finger to her chin. "Except they aren't funny—funny things are done to them—for you and for everyone else they are mean to."

"I think you should leave them alone," Roy said. "You have no idea what they can do."

"You can't apologize for defending yourself," Suki said, putting the mouse back with the others. "Being so afraid can cause all kinds of problems—like stomachaches and hair loss."

Roy knew worrying caused his stomachaches, but he had never heard of the hair problem. "I don't know why I worry so much." Roy subtly ran his fingers through his hair and checked his hand for any strands. Then he glanced over at the bin of wrinkly, bald, pink mice. "I don't like doing things that could get me in trouble or get me hurt—unless it's for some spying adventure."

"Same here," Suki said, "but sometimes you have to take the risk to make things better in your life."

Roy looked down at his old tennis shoes. "That's easy for you to say. I could've pulled that prank on Blob today if I had invisibility spray."

"No, you couldn't," Suki said, unlocking the filing cabinet. "You'd worry about getting caught, so your fear would stop you from ever trying it in the first place."

"I guess you're right." Roy felt his stomach beginning to cramp. "Nicholas thinks I am a wimp too."

"It's not that you're a wimp. It's that your fear is making things worse than they should be." She placed two new-looking bottles on the table. "I know Blob is big and hangs out with the popular jocks, but you've got something he'll never have—and it's not your homework."

"What?"

"You're smart," she said. "That makes Blob mad because he struggles in school, and you remind him that he's not a good student. You're a sixth-grader in an eighth-grade class. He hates that idea and is punishing you for being smart. Trust me, I followed him around at school. He's not hard to figure out. Like you said, he's a blob."

"So, that's what happened to you?" Roy sat in the chair in front of the microscope. "I was wondering why you were being so quiet."

Suki pulled out a bag full of colorful objects from the cabinet. "Yeah, I decided I needed to get more information on him. You know what they say. Keep your friends close and your enemies closer."

Roy was almost jealous of Suki. He would have done anything to be invisible and spy on everyone at school. "So . . . what did you find out?"

"Oh, his locker combination. Who he hangs out with. What he's stolen." Suki sat down next to Roy and put the bag, which was full of balloons, on the table. "You know, the usual stuff."

"He's stolen stuff? How do you know that?"

"Because I found a purse in his locker."

"Wow. He's worse than I thought," Roy said, recalling the rumor he'd heard about Blob being a thief.

"Don't worry, I made things right with my spray. Just like we were talking about."

Roy's stomach cramps got a little more painful. "Oh, no. What did you do?"

"See, there you go again—getting all worried for nothing." Suki pulled a red balloon out of the bag. "When no one was around, I got into his locker and looked through the purse. It was Mrs. Crowley's."

"No way." Roy's anger toward Blob instantaneously increased to the tenth power. Mrs. Crowley was his favorite teacher. "We should probably tell someone."

"Too late. I already took care of it." Suki looked especially proud of herself. "When she got back from lunch, her purse was sitting on her desk."

Roy couldn't believe it. This girl had guts. "I'm sure someone saw the purse floating down the hall."

"No, that's not what I did. I put it under my shirt," Suki explained. "Remember, anything underneath something that is sprayed is invisible too."

"Oh . . . yeah. I see how it would work now."

Suki shook her head. "Your brain makes things much harder than they really are."

Roy shrugged. "Maybe . . . but this whole invisibility thing is new to me, so give me a break."

"Fine, but it's not going to be new for much longer." Suki dangled the red balloon in front of his face.

"What's that supposed to mean? And why are you holding a balloon?"

"It's your turn to do something good and make Blob feel the way he makes others feel."

Roy tried to hide his worried look. "With a balloon?"

"With an invisible balloon . . . filled with water."

Roy let out a nervous laugh. He liked where the idea seemed to be going, but he didn't like the fact that he had to be involved. When it came to his time with Suki, he was learning that he enjoyed being more of a spectator than a participant. "What? Are we going to throw invisible water balloons at him?"

"Not we," Suki said. "You. And you are not going to throw it. You're going to take this balloon." She put it in his hand. "Fill it with water. Spray it." Suki held up the two bottles of spray. "Take it on the bus tomorrow, and put it in the seat behind you."

Roy's heart began to beat faster. "I can't do that. Someone will see me put it there."

"Really? Someone will see it? See what?" Suki said, shoving the first bottle in his other hand. "Stop using the word can't. You can, and you will. You have to."

"I don't have to do what you say."

"Yes...you...do...because I found out something else about Blob today."

Roy was afraid to ask, but he did anyway. "What?"

"He's planning on cornering Nicholas on Halloween night and making him pay for sticking up for you and making him look weak on the bus."

Roy's entire body began to shake. He couldn't say anything.

"He knows where Nicholas lives." Suki looked more serious than Roy had ever seen her. "He's going to secretly follow him around while he's trick-or-treating and play some bad prank on him or get him some other way. He's not sure, but he was talking to Rob about it. He plans on being in costume so no one can blame him for it."

Roy looked at the balloon and the bottles of spray. The situation was no longer about his homework and his feelings. The situation was now about Nicholas, and Roy had no choice but to do something to help his best friend. Maybe Suki had a good idea. Getting Blob before he got to Nicholas seemed like the most logical approach.

"Okay—I'll do it," Roy said.

"You'd better. I'll be watching," Suki said. "Just to be safe, let's do a test run."

"Good idea." Roy looked around. "Where can we get water?"

"Here, give it to me. I'll fill it with the hose outside." Suki left the shed and returned a few moments later with a sagging, bouncy balloon. She tied the opening and held it over the floor. "Don't forget to shake the bottle."

Roy gave the bottle a good shake and then sprayed the entire balloon.

"Once it dries, you'll need to spray the tie really well." Suki passed the balloon to Roy. "Here, it's getting heavy."

Roy held up the balloon and lightly touched it. "I think it's dry enough."

Suki touched it too. "Then you know what to do." She sat down in front of the mice and began tending to them.

Roy worked on the balloon until it was completely sprayed. He walked over to Suki and held it over the bin of mice. "Now, we wait."

"Hey, do you know what's happening on October twenty-eighth?" Suki asked.

Roy knew this was some sort of trick question. It

was probably a famous date when something extraordinary happened, so he thought for a minute.

"Stop thinking about it," Suki said. "You're not going to know." She laughed. "It's my birthday."

"Oh," Roy said, sounding relieved.

"Yep, pretty soon, I'm going to be thirteen." She held her head like a snooty person and flung her hair back. "It sounds so mature, doesn't it?"

"Sort of . . . I guess that's because you'll officially be a teenager."

"Huh . . . a teenager. I like the sound of that."

"Are you going to have a big party?" Roy asked, his arm twitching from holding the balloon.

"I don't know—probably not." Her smile disappeared. "Besides your family and some people at the college, I don't really know anyone here."

"Still, you should have a party. Thirteen seems like a big deal."

Suki patted the almost completely invisible balloon. "I'm sure my mom has something planned. Hey, I completely forgot—we're coming over to your house this weekend."

"Yeah, my mom did say something about that." Roy tried to act nonchalant about the get-together. "You gonna be okay in the sun?"

"We're not coming over until around five-thirty. It should be fine. I'll bring my meter, just in case."

"Meter?"

Suki walked over to an open shelf. She picked up a white, TV-remote-looking thing and showed it to Roy. "This thing. It lets me know the UV ratings around me at all times. I have to take it with me everywhere—except at home, where I know everything has been made safe."

"Oh . . . well, that's good." Roy's arm was totally numb from holding the now invisible balloon.

Suki slid a chair to the middle of the shed. "Put the balloon in the chair, and sit on it."

"No way, I'll get all wet."

"So? You have to test it. That was the whole point of doing it. You're going to go home and get in your pajamas anyway." She took the balloon from his fingers and placed it in the chair. "Don't be such a baby." She pushed the chair closer to him. "Do it."

This girl really enjoyed making a fool of him. But she was right; he had to find out if it would work.

"Here goes nothing."

Roy turned around and aimed his backside at the center of the chair. He felt the balloon flatten, but it didn't pop. He bounced up and down on top of it until, finally—*splish*. Water squirted out in every direction from under his backside.

Suki jumped out of the way. "*Eeehh*—you got me too." She and Roy broke into laughter. "You're going to need to put more water in it. Even though Blob's butt is much bigger than yours."

The laughing got louder when Roy stood up and revealed a giant wet spot on his jeans. "That looks perfect," Suki said.

Roy looked down at the chair. "Wait . . . look . . . you can see the red from the inside of the balloon. What are we going to do about that?"

"Yeah, that could cause some problems," Suki said. "Just blow up the balloon really big and spray it really well. Let it dry, then deflate it, turn it inside out and fill it up with water, then spray the outside of it. Remember, the spray is waterproof. So, the inside should stay invisible too."

"Wow, good idea." Roy picked up one of the red pieces. "Glad we tested it."

"See? I'm bossy for a reason." Suki took a jacket from a hook on the wall. "I know what I'm doing. Here, dry yourself off with this."

Roy patted and rubbed his jeans. "It's no use. I'm soaked. I should go home. It's getting late anyway."

"I'll see you at school tomorrow."

"I guess I won't see you at school tomorrow," Roy said.

"Here." Suki collected the bag of balloons and the two bottles of spray. "Take everything—just in case. And make sure no one sits behind you before Blob gets on the bus. And don't worry. And don't be scared. Don't even think about it. Just do what you have to do."

Roy nodded and headed back toward his house. As he approached the oak tree, he looked down at all the supplies tucked inside his crossed arms. How was he supposed to not think about what he had to do tomorrow? There was so much to figure out. How was he going to keep the seat open behind him? How was he going to get the balloon in the seat without anyone seeing him? What if it rolled off the seat? What if—

Roy reached for the rope, his mind still drowning in questions.

The rope wasn't there.

He looked and felt all around.

It wasn't there.

He tossed all the supplies on the ground and began patting the tree and swinging his arms in the dark.

He couldn't find it.

How could it disappear?

It was there an hour ago.

Then he looked up.

He saw the rope.

But there was a problem—a big loud, annoying problem.

It was Melonie.

She was standing in his open window, dangling and swinging the rope from her hand, so it was just out of Roy's reach.

"Looking for something?" she asked.

CHAPTER 17

BE COOL.

Roy couldn't believe his eyes. He crammed the spray bottle and balloons into his tucked shirt and jumped for the rope. Melonie continued to laugh as she dropped the rope just a few inches out of his reach.

"What's wrong? Too short?" she asked.

"Drop it . . . now," Roy whispered as loud as he could.

"Why should I?" Melonie whispered back. "What are you going to do for me?"

"Do you really want me to tell you what I'm going to do to you if you don't give it to me?" Roy was about to explode. What was his little sister doing in his room? Why was she even awake?

"I think I might go tell Mommy and Daddy," Melonie said. "I'm sure they would love to know that you've been sneaking out of your window at night." Then she pulled the rope into his bedroom and disappeared from the window.

"Mel... wait... come back." Roy's goosebumps started to sweat. "C'mon... what do you want?"

Melonie returned to the window and looked down at Roy. "What have you got?"

Roy looked around. "Well... nothing out here. But if you let me get in my room, I've probably got something I can give you."

"You've got boy stuff. I don't want anything like that."

"Just drop the rope, and we'll figure something out."

"You better figure it out." Melonie flung the rope out the window. "I can still tell Mommy and Daddy—anytime I want."

"Okay," Roy said, grabbing the rope and making his way to the window. He crawled inside and put the rope back out of sight.

"You're in big trouble for using that. There's no fire."

Roy squeezed Melonie's arm. "What are you doing in my room? Do you come in here a lot? How long have you been waiting for me?"

Melonie tried to jerk her arm from Roy's hold.

"None of your business. But I came in tonight because I got scared, and you always seem to be up. You know when I'm scared, I always come to see you."

"There's nothing to be scared about." Roy paused to listen for any signs his parents might have woken up. "I'm watching the house while everyone else is asleep. I'm not going to let anything happen to you, so don't come in here anymore. Got it?"

"Fine. What were you doing across the street anyway?"

"I-I was helping Suki with her math. She does stuff at night—you know, because of her skin thing."

Melonie squinted to see Roy in the moonlight. "What's in your shirt? And why are your pants wet?"

Roy looked down at his bulging belly. "I spilled a glass of water, and this is stuff I borrowed from her for a school project—for science class. You know . . . her dad's a scientist." Roy pulled the bottles and bag of balloons out of his shirt and threw them on the bed.

"That doesn't look like science stuff. I'm gonna tell."

Roy squeezed Melonie's arm harder. "Why do you have to be such a nosey, loud-mouthed brat?" he whisper-yelled. "Why can't you be cool like Nicholas's sister?"

"I'm cool," Melonie whisper-yelled back. "You're

just mean to me, so I am mean back."

"I'm mean to you because you're such a brat. Stop being a brat, and I'll stop being mean. It's that simple. Brothers and sisters are supposed to help each other out—not get each other in trouble."

Melonie's arm went limp in Roy's hand. "So, you'll stop being mean to me if I don't tell?"

"Obviously." Roy let go of Melonie's arm.

"Do I get a prize for not telling?"

"Yeah... you get my trust. Maybe I'll let you do things with me... and tell you secrets."

"The next time you go across the street, can I go with you?"

Ugh, Roy had to think fast. He wasn't about to let his little sister ruin his nights. "We were working on math. You hate math. I don't really like her. I'm just helping her because I feel sorry for her. And I have to go over there late because I have to get my homework done first. And I don't want Mom and Dad to know that I am helping her, or they will try to get me to do more stuff with her. So, I don't want them to know."

Melonie was speechless. Roy grinned on the inside. His explanation had worked, and he was quite proud of himself.

"Fine... but I think you should still have to give me

something," Melonie said.

"I'll give you something, but you have to swear to never tell Mom and Dad—and you can never come in my room again without my permission."

Roy waited for his little sister to respond. He could tell that selfish little brain of hers was picking over a list of girly things he didn't have. She used to be easy to bribe. A corner of his Pop-Tart or half a Twinkie would usually keep her at a tolerable distance—but not anymore. She was getting smarter and more demanding by the day, and outsmarting her was taking more effort than Roy was willing to give.

"I want gummy worms," Melonie said.

Roy looked around his room. "I don't have any."

"The store does."

"Alright, the next time Mom goes to the store, I'll get you some gummy worms with my allowance."

"You have to give me a bag a week."

"That's too much—you'll get cavities, and you'll get in trouble for not brushing your teeth. Plus, I don't get that much allowance, and it'll be hard to hide them from Mom and Dad."

"Then the beginning of every month—I want a bag. That way, we'll both remember our deal. I won't tell, and you won't be mean."

"Deal." Roy tugged Melonie's hand up and down. He bent down and looked right into Melonie's big, blue eyes. "But if you ever tell, I will never forgive you, and I'll be as mean to you as I possibly can. And I will tell my friends to be mean to you. So, be cool."

Melonie looked at the bag of balloons. Roy started to panic again. "Can I have a balloon?"

Roy let out a big sigh of relief. That was the great thing about seven-year-olds—they had a short attention span. "Sure, take a couple. But you didn't get them from me . . . right?"

"No," Melonie said. "I got them from school—they were extras from a science project we did."

"Cool." Roy smiled back. "You should get back to bed."

Melonie took a yellow balloon and a red balloon and skipped toward his door.

"Wait . . . be quiet." Roy poked his head out from behind his door and looked down the hall. "Okay . . . go . . . and don't make a sound."

Melonie tiptoed out the door and then looked back at Roy. "My gummy worms—don't forget."

"I won't," Roy whispered, putting his finger over his mouth and shooing his little sister down the hall.

Roy shut his door and sat on the bed. He was

exhausted. His mind wanted to worry about Melonie and her big mouth, but there wasn't time. He changed into his pajamas and got busy.

He picked out a red balloon, blew it up really big, and tied the end. Then he placed it on the center of his desk. He gave the first spray a good shake and aimed the nozzle right at the balloon, only to jerk the bottle back when he realized he wasn't thinking clearly. He couldn't just spray this stuff anywhere—he had to be careful.

He cracked his door and checked for any movement. Keeping one eye on his parent's bedroom door, he snuck into the bathroom with all the supplies.

Once locked inside, he placed the balloon in the sink and sprayed it just like he had done in the lab. Between sprays, he sat on the toilet and listened to the quiet.

After what seemed like hours and hours, the sink eventually looked empty. Roy felt for the balloon and found the tie. He dug his fingernail under the taut rubber loop and pinched and pulled. The tie unwound, and the balloon flew out of his hands and puttered through the air.

Pppppssssssssshhhhhh—splat. Even though the noise sounded like something you might hear coming from a bathroom, Roy stopped breathing and listened for any signs of a stirring family member.

All was quiet.

Roy felt around on the cold tile floor in search of the deflated balloon. As he got closer to the toilet, he noticed a weird dimpling in the water. Of course, Roy should have known the balloon would land in the worst possible place. He considered flushing it and starting over, but then he thought about how much time he would have to spend making another one invisible.

Roy had no choice. He held his breath, reached into the toilet, grabbed the balloon, and tossed it into the sink. Once thoroughly rinsed, Roy poked his finger into the hole to turn the balloon inside out. The red began to appear as the stretchy material covered Roy's finger. Before long, he was holding a completely visible, red balloon.

He wrapped the open end of the balloon around the faucet and turned on the water. It began to stretch and droop. He filled it to twice the size of the test balloon. Then he tied it tight and placed it back in the sink. He sprayed it just like before and waited. A few minutes later, Roy was holding a cold, floppy, invisible water balloon just waiting to burst onto Blob's backside.

He scrubbed the sink and gathered up all the supplies. After he crept back to his room, he hid the bottles and placed the balloon next to his book bag on the floor.

Roy was so tired that he fell into bed.

CHAPTER 18

LIKE MAGIC.

"You're going to be late." Roy opened his eyes to find his mom stroking his hair. "You were fast asleep. That must have been some good dream you were having." She collected his dirty clothes off the floor. "Next time, laundry basket—okay? Hurry up. You don't want to miss the bus."

Thump. Thump. Thump. His mom dragged the laundry hamper downstairs.

Roy sprung out of bed. He rubbed his eyes. He had to get his brain working. There was too much to do, and no mistakes could be made.

Laundry—it was laundry day. Roy dropped to the floor and retrieved his invisible shoe from behind his secret treasure box. He crammed it deep into his pack. He got dressed and felt around for the balloon until he found the knotted end.

How do you hide something jiggly, heavy, and invisible? he wondered.

Roy looked out his window. It was a gray and cold-looking day with a shower of leaves catching a ride on the morning breeze. He was sure his mom would insist he wear a jacket. He found the biggest one in his closet and draped it over his arm, which hid his clenched hand holding the balloon.

He proceeded downstairs and placed everything by the back door. His mom seemed to smile at the fact that she didn't have to remind him that it was cold outside. While she and Melonie were busy talking in the kitchen, Roy pulled the shoe from his pack and dropped it into the washing machine.

Right as he heard the bus turning onto his street, he took his last bite of breakfast and ran out of the house before his mom and Melonie had a chance to say "goodbye." Roy was the last kid to arrive at the corner. After claiming his and Nicholas's regular spot, he put his pack at his feet and placed the balloon in his lap like it was some priceless, prehistoric egg. He draped his jacket across the back of the seat.

Just like he anticipated, a sharp turn onto Nicholas's street sent his jacket sliding and landing on the floor behind him. So far, so good, he thought.

Now, for the tricky part. When the bus greeted the group of waiting kids, Roy got up from his seat and dropped his left arm by his side, with the balloon dangling from his pinched fingers. He placed the balloon in the seat behind him while he picked up his jacket. He made sure to turn his back to the kids across the aisle so they could not see his movements.

Roy returned to his seat right as Nicholas approached the aisle. "What were you doing?" Nicholas asked, taking the spot next to him.

Roy shrugged and answered, "My jacket fell off the back of the seat. I brought it so my mom wouldn't nag me. I wasn't in the mood."

Nicholas smiled. "Yeah, mine's in my backpack."

As the bus started to roll, Roy pretended to listen to his friend. But all he could think about was the floppy, invisible balloon that could tumble to the floor at any second.

"You gonna give you-know-who your notebook today?" Nicholas asked, breaking Roy's concentration.

"Huh? Oh . . . no. I don't think I'll have to today," Roy said, watching the door smack open at the next stop.

Nicholas looked toward the door as well. "What do

you mean—you don't think so?"

Roy watched the kids load onto the bus. "Just what I said . . . I'm not worried about it."

"You're acting weird. What—"

"I wouldn't sit there," Roy said to a kid turning into the seat behind him. "That mean guy will just make you move."

The kid thanked Roy for reminding him and took the next seat down. Nicholas looked right at Roy. "Why'd you do that?"

"I know what I'm doing." Roy turned around and looked at the seat. There was actually an indentation where the balloon was still sitting.

Nicholas looked at the seat too. "What are you looking at?"

Roy didn't say anything. He wished he could tell his friend about Blob's Halloween plan and about how he was trying to stop him. But telling Nicholas some things would only lead to other things, and Roy couldn't tell him everything, so he decided to tell him nothing.

The bus squealed up to the next stop—Blob's stop. Roy stared Blob down as he entered the bus with Rob right behind him.

"Want a picture?" Blob snarled. Roy kept on staring.

Blob held out his arm in front of Nicholas's face and snapped at Roy. "Notebook . . . hand it over." Blob turned and scooted behind Nicholas. He leaned over the boys. "Now."

Roy turned around and looked up at Blob. Rob pushed Blob toward the window so he could sit down. Blob continued to snarl at Roy as his behind made its way closer to the seat. Roy kept staring back, making sure to not take his eyes off him until he was perfectly positioned over the balloon.

"I'm not telling you again, Tinkleweenie." Blob flicked Roy's hair and plunked down on the seat.

Faaawiiiiiiiiish. Water spewed out from underneath Blob's buns and between his legs. Roy felt a few drops land on his head.

Blob grabbed the seat back behind Roy, arched his back, and jumped up. "What the—" He looked back at the seat.

Rob leaped back into the aisle.

Everyone in the back of the bus began laughing at Blob's soaking wet behind. There was so much water that his lap was almost equally soaked.

The bus pulled up to the last stop. Blob pushed Rob out of the way and plowed over the kids going up the stairs. The entire bus was laughing and pointing. Roy even saw the bus driver smirk as Blob went running down the sidewalk.

Roy let out a silent sigh of relief.

HE DID IT.

HE ACTUALLY DID IT.

IT. FELT. SO. GOOD.

Rob looked at his wet legs and made it off the bus right before the door closed.

The bus driver looked in his mirror at all the kids. "Everyone okay back there?"

Roy yelled loud enough to be heard over all the laughter. "Everything's fine. He had an accident."

The bus roared even louder as it took off for school. Nicholas looked back at the puddles of water on the seat and floor. Then he looked at Roy. "What did you do?" he asked with a look of awe.

"What? I didn't do anything."

Nicholas kept grinning. "Yeah, sure you didn't. C'mon, tell me. How'd you do it?"

Roy looked around. "Can't tell you now."

"When?" Nicholas said, still staring at the seat in wonder.

"Later, when it's safe," Roy whispered. "Don't tell anyone it was me."

Nicholas gave a slight nod. The rest of the ride

couldn't have been better. Everyone was laughing and giggling as they got off the bus. It was a rare sight, and Roy was proud to be the one that had made everyone happy.

He jumped onto the sidewalk from the last bus step. He puffed his chest out and started walking toward the sixth-grade wing with his best friend.

Then Roy remembered. Suki—he had forgotten all about her. Did she see everything?

"C'mon, you can tell me now," Nicholas said, nudging Roy as they walked to class.

Roy looked around. But he wasn't looking to see if it was safe to tell Nicholas. Instead, he was listening for any sounds from Suki.

"Please, I'm your best friend. You have to tell me." Nicholas pulled his friend's arm and stopped him from entering Mrs. Scarsdale's room.

"I can't tell you how I did it," Roy said. "It was a type of magic—like magician magic."

"Huh? I didn't know you did magic."

"Yeah, I've gotten some magic kits over the years and practiced some tricks. You're just going to have to trust me."

"But you can tell me."

"Magicians don't tell how their tricks are done.

That's rule number one that all magicians have to stick to. If not, then there would be no magic."

Nicholas squinted with uncertainty.

Baaariiiiing.

"That's the first bell. We'd better go," Roy said. He pulled away and walked into class. He didn't care if he had confused his friend. He only cared that Nicholas knew he had pranked Blob.

As they took their seats, the room was humming with gossip about Blob's bus accident. Roy and Nicholas said nothing.

Blob was a no-show in math class, and Roy had not heard a peep out of Suki. Unlike Nicholas's brave bus confrontation with the biggest guy at the school, Blob's so-called accident had made its way to the eighth-grade wing. Roy was a little frustrated that he couldn't take credit for the prank, but he was glad Blob had been put in his place and, hopefully, had learned his lesson.

By the end of the day, the stories had reached epic proportions.

"I heard his bladder sprung a leak," one kid said on the bus, looking at the empty seat now dry from the sun. "That's what happens when you hold it too long."

"No way, I'm never gonna sit there," another kid

said. "That's the icky seat."

"I heard he has some kind of disease," an eighth-grader added.

"I hear you can get that way if you drink too much soda. That's why my mom doesn't let me drink the stuff."

Roy and Nicholas listened and laughed the entire bus ride home. It had been the best middle-school day ever. Roy was happy, and his best friend was happy. And that's the way it should always be.

As he walked away from the bus stop, Roy looked back at Suki's house. Where was she? He hoped she hadn't missed everything.

Once at home, Roy snuck one of his dad's sodas from the fridge and went straight to his room. Next to his bed sat his recently washed, fully-visible tennis shoe. He placed it beside the other one in the closet and did a back leap onto his bed.

Suki was definitely the smartest kid he had ever known. Without her help, he could have never stopped Blob from taking his homework or won back the respect of Nicholas.

He should probably let her know that.

CHAPTER 19

REALLY?

Later that night, when he opened the door to the lab, the look on Suki's face said it all.

"See? I told you not to worry," Suki said. She pulled Roy inside and locked the door behind him. "You were amazing. And the way you explained it to your friend . . . pure genius. Thanks for not telling. I got a little worried for a minute."

"I told you," Roy said as he sat down and placed all the supplies he had borrowed back on the table. "I can keep a secret. Especially when it's not mine to tell."

"Yeah, you've proven that for sure. And don't worry, your secret is safe with me too."

"Hey, why didn't you say anything at school today?"

Suki sat down next to him. "Because it was your prank, and I didn't want to make you nervous. I know I can make you even more worried. You had a lot on your mind without me bothering you."

"What did you do all day without Blob to follow around?"

"I did what anyone would do if they were invisible. I listened in on all the kids' and teachers' conversations. And I sat in on a Spanish class and a social studies class—so I wouldn't have to learn that stuff on my own."

"Did you find out anything interesting?"

Suki looked ready to talk. "Teachers gossip more than kids."

"Really?" Roy sat on his hands and examined Suki's face for any signs that he should be concerned.

"Yeah, they have students they like and ones they don't."

"Huh..." Roy stared off into space and ran down his list of teachers.

Suki put her hand on Roy's shoulder. "Don't worry... from what I saw, most of the teachers like you."

"Did you hear anything bad about me—like from other kids?"

"Nah, but I hung out in the eighth-grade wing the most. They talk about much more interesting stuff."

"Like . . . what?

"How much this person likes that person. You know, mushy stuff." Suki got up and took her binoculars off the wall hook. "I think the whole girlfriend-boyfriend thing is a waste of time. Who needs it? Let's go around front and do some spying."

Roy followed Suki to the front yard. He was happy to end the conversation.

They both got comfortable on a blanket of leaves under the big tree. With her best pair of binoculars, Suki scanned Roy's side of the street from right to left. "This is the deadest place I have ever lived."

Roy watched Suki as she searched for something interesting to look at. If he could no longer have Bart as a neighbor, Suki was the perfect person to fill the void. As far as he was concerned, she was the most interesting person in his life. And not because of the invisibility spray.

He wondered if Suki found him interesting.

Probably not, he thought. But he was working on it.

No matter what, it was a good thing she hadn't moved to the neighborhood this past summer. She would have blown everything for him and Bart. Roy often thought life had lousy timing. Like when his parent's vacation plans collided with his and Bart's plans, almost spoiling one of the greatest opportunities of his life. Luckily, everything had worked out because they had been able to bypass life's cruel sense of humor and manipulate the timing to work for them.

But, for once, life seemed to get it right; the timing felt harmonious. Bart left. Suki arrived. Things couldn't have worked out better.

"Here, let me see," Roy said, taking the binoculars and aiming them down the street. "That white house, way down there at the corner . . ." Roy lowered the binoculars and whispered extra soft. "Everyone thinks it's haunted."

Suki took the binoculars back. "Where?"

Roy guided the binoculars to the right of where she was looking. "The other corner. It's hard to see from here—especially in the dark."

"That place?" Suki whispered with a snort-laugh. "Why would people think it's haunted?"

"Rumor has it that a couple of kids snuck into the house and never came out. And now they haunt the place. But I don't believe it," Roy said. "I think people make up stories about the house because it's empty and kind of rundown."

"No way anything like that happened in this neighborhood." Suki adjusted the binoculars for a sharper view. "That's why my parents decided to move here. I'd better make sure they never hear that story because they would move someplace else, for sure."

"I'm not going to say anything." Roy tried not to worry about the possibility of Suki moving. "And you're right. Nothing ever happens here."

"Let's go down there and check it out." Suki jumped up, ready to spy.

"Are you kidding me?" Roy stood up and blocked her from taking off down the street. "We can't do that—someone's going to see us."

Suki looked around. "Really? Who? Who is going to see us?"

"You never know," Roy whispered, pulling Suki back behind the tree. "I mean . . . we're spying and up late. What makes you think someone else isn't doing exactly what we're doing? They could be looking at us right now."

"Fine. I know how to fix that." Suki walked back toward the shed.

Roy didn't follow immediately. Not all of Suki's ideas were good.

After a few seconds, Roy ran after her. She was already in the shed, feeling around for something in the front right corner. "I'll wear my school gear."

"Not tonight," Roy said, reaching out to stop her. As much as he thought the house probably wasn't haunted, he wasn't prepared to find out tonight; he'd heard some pretty scary stuff about the place.

"Why? Tomorrow's Saturday. It's not like you have to get up early or something."

"Yeah... but remember, all of us are getting together tomorrow afternoon, and I know my mom is going to get me up early to run errands."

"Errands?" Suki chuckled.

"It's not like I have a choice—she makes me go," Roy said, knowing he actually wanted to go with his mom tomorrow. He needed to get Suki a birthday present and, of course, gummy worms for Melonie. "Besides, it's not that bad... a lot of times she gets me things I want."

"I guess I get it," she said. "That's one good thing about having XP. My parents don't drag me around much during the day while they do their boring, adult stuff."

"If you say so." Roy looked at his watch. "Um... I'd better get going. Thanks for helping me with Blob." Roy looked at his feet. "You have some really smart ideas."

"No problem." Suki looked at her feet. "Thanks for

making my idea look so good."

"I guess I'll see you tomorrow at my house—during the day. Oh . . . and don't forget your binoculars . . . for looking at the sky."

"Oh . . . I won't," she said. "Should we act like we aren't friends?"

Roy thought for a few seconds. "I think we should act like we aren't friends yet, but we could be some day."

Suki agreed.

Roy closed the shed door and took off toward the fire escape. He wasn't about to tell Suki that Melonie had caught him sneaking out. He couldn't. It was too embarrassing.

Even with the possibility of his little sister blabbing about his nights across the street, he was looking forward to the barbecue. Anything cooked on a grill was his favorite kind of food. But before he could enjoy the day, he had to get the fattest gummy worms he could find so that Melonie's big mouth would be too stuffed to tell on him. He also had to buy Suki's gift without the rest of the Winklesteens figuring out it was a gift.

It was going to be a busy Saturday.

CHAPTER 20

AHH . . .

Roy was right. His mom had him up bright and early to run errands. She even made his dad come.

"When we get to the shopping center, we'll split up into teams," his mom said as they all piled into the family car. "Charles, you and Roy will go to the hardware store to get some lamp oil and some new tiki torches, and—here, just take the list." She stuffed the piece of paper into her husband's shirt pocket. "Melonie and I will run to the home store for a few things, and we'll meet at the grocery store. Sound good, everyone?" She looked back at Roy and Melonie. They both nodded and ignored each other for the rest of the ride.

Once at the hardware store, Charles Winklesteen concentrated on his wife's list while Roy looked around at all the stuff on the shelves. Typically, he wouldn't think of getting a gift for a girl from a store that sold mostly tools and lumber. But Suki was different. She had a science lab, a box full of fossils, and bigger binoculars than he had.

When they got to the lightbulb aisle, Roy noticed a flashlight display. He picked out a black one and examined it. Perfect, he thought. Suki's flashlight barely worked, and every spy needed a reliable flashlight.

He checked the price and then fumbled through his wallet. He had enough money to cover the flashlight and Melonie's gummy worms, especially if he used all the quarters he had.

He inspected all the black flashlights until he found the one that looked like it had gotten the least amount of human contact. When he returned to his dad's side, Roy held the flashlight up. "I'm gonna get this with my own money."

His dad took the flashlight and gave it a quick test. "You don't need to waste your money. I might have an extra one you can have. What do you need a flashlight for anyway?"

Roy hadn't thought his dad would ask so many questions, especially since he always bought something for himself at any home improvement store. He had so many tools that Roy was certain he hadn't used all of them. "I like it," Roy explained. "It's small but bright. And shouldn't I have a flashlight... you know... for emergencies?"

Roy gave his father a serious look. He knew that any action regarding safety and security was always going to get his parents' approval. Charles and Helen Winklesteen were all about that kind of stuff.

Roy's dad grinned and said, "You're right, it is cool." He handed the light back to Roy. "And it never hurts to be prepared. You could spend your money on a lot worse, I guess."

With all the items checked off the list, Roy and his dad met up with his mom and Melonie in the crowded grocery store. Melonie immediately demanded Roy's attention. "My gummies, they're in aisle six. Don't forget," she whispered.

"I'm gonna go over there," Roy said, gesturing to aisle six as he walked away from the rest of his family. He gave Melonie a stern look as he disappeared out of her view. His parents were too busy figuring out what kind of cheese went with barbecue to notice he had walked away.

Roy picked up the cheapest bag of gummy worms he

could find. On the way back to his parents, he passed the section with floral bouquets, plants, and balloons and noticed a big bucket of smiling sunflowers. One of those would make Suki's gift even better. He looked over the entire bunch and pulled out the biggest, brightest one. He put it in one of the complimentary bags and met up with his parents.

"Roy, where have you been?" his mom asked, tossing more cheese into the basket. "What's that you've got?" She peeped into the bag. "A sunflower... you're getting a sunflower?"

Roy had already figured out what he was going to say. "Oh... we have to draw a flower for art... so I thought this would be the easiest. And we can't use a picture to draw from."

"Do you have to draw gummy worms too?" his dad asked, tugging on the bag in Roy's other hand. "Let me guess, you can't use a picture to draw those either." Roy's mom chuckled and returned to her shopping. His dad shrugged his shoulders. "It's your money."

"You've got a lot in your hands, Roy. You want me to hold those for you?" Melonie said, yanking the bag of gummies.

Roy lifted them out of her reach. "No, for now, they're safest in my hands. Maybe if you are nice, I'll give you one—deal?"

"Fine." Melonie buried her face in her mother's sweater.

With a basket full of all things barbecue and then some, the Winklesteen family finally purchased their items and returned home.

As he ran up the stairs to his room, Roy barely heard his mom call out from the kitchen, "We're setting up in the backyard in a few minutes. We'll need your help."

Roy closed his door and laid out everything he had bought. He was searching for a container to put the sunflower in when Melonie banged on his door. "Roy? Oh . . . Roooyyy."

He opened his door with the gummies behind his back. "Once you take this bag, you're sworn to secrecy. If you break the vow of silence, bad things will happen."

Melonie's blue eyes looked more confused than ever. "Huh?"

"Here." Roy pushed the bag into her stomach. "We have a deal. Don't tell, and don't let Mom and Dad see the worms. Remember, be cool."

Melonie let out a squeal while she struggled to get the bag open. "Deal, as long as I get my gummies."

"No more until next month," Roy reminded her.

Melonie nodded as she wrapped her teeth around the green end of a worm, pulling on it until it snapped in half. "I wouldn't eat them all at once. A month is a long time." Roy pushed his sister away from his door. "Go find a place to hide them."

Melonie took off down the hall, and Roy returned to his purchases. He filled his pencil cup with water from the bathroom sink and placed the parched-looking sunflower in the center of it. He had to lean the flower against his desk lamp to keep the whole thing from falling over.

Pleased with his effort, he turned his attention to the flashlight. He needed something to wrap it in. He knew where his mom kept the pretty paper, but that was too easy. He wanted to be clever because he knew that's what Suki would do.

He reached under his bed and pulled out his box of secret treasures. He opened it up and felt around until he was able to find the invisible piece of paper. He uncrumpled it and flattened it on his desk with the visible side up. He positioned the flashlight in the center of it, rolled everything up like a burrito, and twisted the ends. Invisible wrapping paper was the best, Roy thought. It was impossible to criticize a person's wrapping skills when no one could see it.

He placed the invisible package in his desk drawer right below the sunflower. Suki's birthday was the day after next, and he couldn't wait to surprise her with everything.

He joined his family in the backyard. The day was proving to be unusually warm, and the sun was unapologetically bright. Roy wasn't worried, though. Suki might have been a risk-taker with some things but not with her skin. Besides, her parents wouldn't let her come over if there was the slightest chance of the sun getting to her.

The girls worked in the kitchen, his dad tended to the grill, and Roy wiped down all the furniture and set up the torches. Then he draped an electric blue cloth across the picnic table and arranged a bucket of ice and beverages on another table with an umbrella. The entire family worked together to bring out all the platters and bowls filled with enough food to feed both families for a month, which was fine with Roy.

After completing every item on his mom's to-do list, the entire Winklesteen family stepped back for a few seconds to admire their work. The yard had a sophisticated but welcoming feel. Suki was bound to be impressed.

Right as Roy checked his watch, he heard the faint

chime of the doorbell. He stayed in the backyard with the food while the rest of his family went to the door. He didn't want to appear too excited to see the neighbor he wasn't supposed to know very well.

Once everyone was outside, Suki jogged right to Roy, who was sitting at the picnic table eating as many deviled eggs as he could before his mom insisted that he share. She looked uncomfortably warm in her outfit, but he kept his cool and didn't say anything.

They sat next to each other but avoided making a lot of eye contact. It wasn't hard for Roy to act like he didn't really know Suki. He could barely see her face from underneath the hat, face shield, and sunglasses. She was somewhere underneath all those layers, but he was struggling to find the opinionated, bossy know-it-all he had come to know—and like. It was as though all the stuff she had to wear covered up her personality too. It wasn't fair, Roy thought. He understood, more than any time before, why Suki's grandmother was so determined to help her.

Suki kept a vigilant eye on her UV meter. As soon as the number dropped to ten, she took off as much of her clothing and accessories as being in the presence of others would allow. "Ahh . . . that's better." She closed her eyes and tilted her face toward the sky.

Out of respect for Suki and her condition, everyone had waited to officially dig into the feast. Roy didn't mind. He had snarfed down enough eggs to quiet his rumbling stomach. But once she was free from all the coverings, both families filled their plates and found a comfortable spot to enjoy the slight but very welcome breeze.

"Don't you hate wearing all that stuff?" Melonie asked, looking at the pile of clothing Suki was struggling to fold into a tote bag she had brought.

"Cram it, Mel," Roy said. "Don't be rude."

"No, it's okay," Suki said, brushing her slightly rumpled hair with her fingers. "There's nothing wrong with asking."

"Yeah, Roy." Melonie shot her brother an I'm-smarter-than-you-think look.

Suki kicked her bag. "I hate wearing all of it . . . and putting on sunscreen all the time. But I'm used to it because I've always had to do it."

"I feel sad for you," Melonie said. "I'm sorry the sun is so mean to you."

Suki showed Roy's little sister a lot more patience than she had ever shown Roy. "It's not your fault, and don't feel sorry for me. I'm fine."

Melonie grinned and bit into her chicken leg. Suki

and Roy ate until they both looked blissfully sick. So far, it had been a successful barbecue.

"Look," Roy said, pointing at the sky. "The first visible star of the night."

Suki looked up. "Except, that's not a star, it's Venus—but good try anyway."

Roy squinted. "How do you know that?"

"Well, for one thing, stars twinkle, and it's not twinkling. And, second, I looked at my astronomy chart right before we came here."

"So, you know it all because you have all the stuff that helps you know it all." Roy elbowed her arm, relieved to see that the quiet Suki had disappeared with all the extra clothing.

"Yeah, I'm a know-it-all. Stick with me, and you could be one too." She elbowed him back.

The two of them spent the rest of the night comparing views through their binoculars. Melonie flitted back and forth between the grown-ups and the big kids, keeping her mouth shut about what she thought she knew about Suki and Roy. Everyone was happy and laughing, and no one seemed to want the night to end.

So, of course, the night had to end.

"I'm sorry we have to cut the evening short," Mrs.

Moore said as she retrieved her empty container that had been full of brownies. "It's so beautiful out here, and thanks for making us feel so welcome."

"Do we have to go now?" Suki asked, giving her mom her saddest puppy dog eyes.

"I'm afraid we do," Mrs. Moore said. "We have to get up early so we can be at Aunt Ivy's house by noon. Your cousins are looking forward to celebrating your birthday with you, and you know we have to see the doctor."

"Happy early birthday, Suki," Roy's dad said. "We'll watch the house while you're gone."

"Gone." That was all Roy heard and thought about for the next few minutes. Why hadn't she told him she was going out of town? It seemed kind of important. He would have told her.

He drifted back into the conversation just in time to hear when the Moores were planning on returning.

Roy sighed.

What was he going to do until Tuesday?

CHAPTER 21

LOSER.

Later that night, Roy sat at his desk and peered out his window. Suki's house was dark, and even though he couldn't see it, he knew her lab was dark too. That's because everyone in the Moore family was getting their rest for the busy days ahead. They had relatives to visit, a big birthday to celebrate, and a doctor to see.

Roy felt bad. He had been impatient and uncaring toward Suki. XP was much more serious than he'd imagined. Seeing what she had to go through just to attend a late afternoon barbecue made him understand her better. It wasn't easy being her, and he should never forget that.

He looked at the sunflower. He hoped it would stay bright and open long enough to give to his new friend.

As for his best friend, he and Nicholas got together

the next day. They were having so much fun that it felt like they were back in elementary school. The balloon incident had gained Roy a lot of respect, and their friendship seemed stronger than ever.

"C'mon," Nicholas said. "You can show me your magic tricks now. We're in your room. Who's gonna see?"

"I can't." Roy stood firmly. "Magic wouldn't be magic if magicians told their best friends how they did their tricks. Sorry, it is what it is."

"So, you planning any other tricks?"

"You'll see."

Nicholas laughed. "Man, I'm actually looking forward to riding the bus now."

Roy joined in Nicholas's laughter, but he knew the truth. He didn't have any more tricks to pull on Blob. Certainly, the busting balloon had embarrassed the big guy enough to not want to draw any attention to himself. Maybe he was so humiliated that he would never ride the bus again. Maybe he would never come to school again. Maybe he would move out of the neighborhood. Maybe—just maybe, Roy wished.

But, like most of Roy's wishes, this one didn't come true.

Monday morning, Blob *plomped* up the bus stairs

louder than ever. His face was red, but not from embarrassment. His angry look dared anyone to laugh at him. He seemed taller and more muscular than ever before. Roy swore he saw at least three more chest hairs peeking out from under his collar.

Everyone on the bus was silent. They all knew that the slightest snicker might set Blob off. He passed by Roy and Nicholas and started to turn into the seat behind them.

"What are you doing?" Rob asked, yanking on his jacket. "I'm not sitting there."

Blob looked down at the seat, growled, and then pushed Rob into the seat across the aisle.

Roy felt a wadded-up piece of paper bounce off his head. "Throw it here, Tinkleweenie—now."

Nicholas looked at Roy. He was waiting for something hilarious to happen. The whole bus seemed to be holding their breath . . . waiting.

But nothing happened. Roy had nothing and didn't know what to do. He was no magician. He was nothing without Suki and her invisibility spray, and when he tossed his notebook across the aisle to Blob, the entire bus knew he was nothing—especially his best friend. But he had to do it. If not for him, for Nicholas. Roy knew that the angrier Blob got, the more likely he would follow through with his Halloween plans.

"I wouldn't give it to him," Nicholas yelled as he stared Blob in the eyes. "He'll probably get it all wet."

The entire bus roared with laughter.

Blob sprung up from his seat and lunged at Nicholas. He yanked his collar and threw him to the floor. "You're dead, loser." Blob straddled Nicholas's body and raised his clenched hand.

The bus squealed to a stop, and the driver headed toward the commotion. "Get off him," he said. Then he pushed Blob back onto the seat. He pulled Nicholas to his feet and sat him back down next to Roy. He looked straight at Blob. "Do anything like that again, and it'll be the last time you ride my bus."

The driver returned to his seat and continued to the school. Roy and Nicholas sat in silence. It was the worst day of Roy's life.

If only he could disappear.

The silence continued for the entire school day and the bus ride home. No rumors were spreading about the incident. Nicholas wasn't talking to Roy. Roy was too afraid to talk to Nicholas, and Blob was too angry to talk to anyone.

The trick had made a bad situation even worse.

The following morning, the silence and anger

continued. Nicholas passed right by Roy on the bus and sat with some of his new friends in the back.

Roy was sitting alone when Blob stepped onto the bus.

He laughed and tapped Rob on the back. "Would you look here ... must be trouble in paradise. Hey, Tinkleweenie, did you and your girlfriend break up?"

Rob laughed and slid into the same seat as yesterday. Blob didn't follow him. Instead, he sat down right next to Roy. "Well, isn't this convenient?" Blob said. "You know the drill ... hand it over." Roy felt sick and lightheaded. He couldn't move. "I'm not telling you again." Blob kicked Roy's backpack.

Roy leaned over and unzipped his bag. He could feel the stares from everyone on the bus. Nicholas's stare was incredibly painful. Roy pulled out his notebook. Blob snatched it out of his hands, stood up, and turned around to face Nicholas. "C'mon, I dare ya," Blob said, waving the notebook back and forth.

Roy and Nicholas caught eyes briefly before Nicholas returned to the conversation with his friends.

Nicholas stayed away from Roy for the rest of the day. Who could blame him? Blob was out to get him, and it was all Roy's fault.

The only person that wanted to sit next to Roy on

the bus ride home was the girl that always sat behind the driver.

"You can sit here," she said. Her smile presented a mouth full of metal. "No one will bother you."

Roy looked around. Nicholas was already at the back, surrounded by his friends who appeared to be protecting him. Blob was watching and waiting for Roy to sit alone in his usual seat.

With no better option to choose from, he sat down next to her and smiled. "Thanks," he said.

As the bus made the sharp right turn out of the school driveway, one thing was clear—Roy was on his own.

CHAPTER 22

FINALLY.

Roy hid out in his room after school. He didn't bother looking out his window because there was nothing to see. He laid his head on his desk and studied the drooping sunflower. It looked how he felt.

When 10:45 p.m. finally glowed on his watch, Roy couldn't wait any longer. He grabbed Suki's gifts and practically fell down the fire escape. As he opened the gate to the Moores' backyard, he was relieved to see the light glowing through the shed window.

When Roy opened the door, Suki spun around with a startled look. "You're early," she said. She held up her arm and pointed to the red band around her wrist. "I got a watch for my birthday."

Roy gave Suki a big smile. "Nice..." He walked over to her to get a closer look. "I wasn't sure you were going to be here."

"We got back this afternoon," she said, noticing the flower. "Glad to see me?"

Roy shrugged and tried to stay calm. "Sure."

"What's that?"

"Oh... it's for you." Roy reached his arm out toward Suki. "It's a sunflower. You know... since you can't go in the sun—I thought this would be—"

"Yeah... I get it. Thanks." She put the flower in a glass of water sitting next to her microscope. "There, it looks like it needs it worse than I do."

"Sorry it's droopy." Roy pulled the wrapped flashlight from his back pocket. "When I got it, I didn't know you'd be gone for a few days."

"That's okay. I guess I should have said something."

"By the way, happy birthday. Here's the rest of your present." Roy held out his open palm.

Suki looked at Roy's empty, open hand. "Aw... that's so sweet—you got me nothing."

They both laughed. "No, it's wrapped in the paper—you know—from the first night you showed me the spray."

Suki felt around in Roy's hand. She clutched the package and unrolled it in her other hand. "Wow—thanks." Her face lit up. "I need a new one of these."

"Yeah, I know," Roy said, studying Suki's reaction. "This one is really good. And it's small . . . which is perfect for spying. You just turn the top a little, and it comes on."

"Let's test it out." Suki flipped off the shed light. "You're right . . . this is perfect for spying. It really lights up the place." Suki moved the light around the room until it lit up the center of Roy's face. "Whoa, you look kinda wicked."

Roy made a scary face. Suki laughed and then shined the light on her face. He could see a slight shadow on her neck from her scar. "Sorry my sister was so stupid at the barbecue."

"What do you mean?"

"You know . . . her dumb question—about you having to wear all that stuff."

"Uh . . . I don't care." Suki turned the shed light back on and placed the flashlight on the table. "I don't mind answering questions. But I hate the stares."

"I guess," Roy began. "I wish you didn't have to wear all that stuff. I had no idea you were suffering from such a bad disorder."

"Suffering?" she said. "Do I look like I'm suffering?"

"Well . . . no . . . but—"

"Nothing about me is suffering." Suki threw out her

arms. "I mean, yeah, I was born with this disorder. I've had it my whole life. But I'm living with it... not suffering from it."

Roy sat down in the other chair. "Okay... sorry. But I didn't really understand what XP was... until I saw what you had to do just to be outside in the sun... for a little while. I guess I feel bad for not understanding what it was all about."

"Don't feel bad. It's not your fault, and it's not your problem." Suki gave Roy's leg a gentle kick. "I'm fine."

"Okay, then... I won't feel bad."

Suki admired her flashlight. "We need to put this to good use." She got up and peeped out the door. "C'mon, follow me."

"Where are we going?"

"We're gonna go check out that alleged haunted house."

"We can't. What if someone sees us?" Roy tried to stop Suki from taking a step into the yard. "It's trespassing, you know. There's even a sign on the front door that says, 'No Trespassing.' I think that means we could go to jail if we get caught."

"Fine, then no one will see us." Suki felt around in the back corner. "Here, put this on."

She was obviously holding something, but Roy

couldn't see it. "What am I putting on?"

"Some of my invisible gear I use to go to your school. I made extra."

Roy began fumbling around with all the clothes. It was hard getting dressed when you couldn't see what you were putting on. But after a few minutes, he sort of got the hang of it.

After they inspected each other for any visible areas, Suki secured her new flashlight in her pants pocket, and they tiptoed to the front yard. Roy could hear Suki shuffling about. Somehow, her invisibility seemed different from when she was at school. Maybe the dark street, dotted with porch lights and Halloween decorations, had something to do with it. The night had a way of sprinkling a little bit of eerie on even the most ordinary moments. The fact that Roy was standing next to an invisible person in the middle of the night sent a chill down his spine—but in a good way.

Then it dawned on him—he was invisible too. Wow. He never thought he would ever—

"Let's go," Suki said, taking a step onto the sidewalk.

Roy honed in on her footsteps and followed close behind. He began to worry. What if the rumors about the house were true? What if it was haunted? Ghosts were invisible, and he and Suki were invisible. Would the ghosts think they were ghosts?

"So, did the balloon embarrass Blob enough to leave you alone?" Roy heard Suki whisper.

He didn't want to tell her what had really happened, but he needed to tell someone, and she was the only one around. "It was awful," Roy started. "The balloon made him angrier. He's worse than ever before. If the bus driver hadn't stopped him, he would have shredded Nicholas to pieces."

"Why? Did Nicholas stick up for you again?"

"I guess." Roy's voice got much softer. "Everything is all messed up now. I don't see the big deal in giving him my notebook—it's just homework. Nicholas doesn't have to be in a class with him—or even go to the eighth-grade wing. He doesn't get it."

"So, he's mad at you?"

"He's not talking to me, sitting on the bus with me, or eating lunch with me."

"He wants you to stick up for yourself."

"He wanted me to pull another trick on Blob. But I didn't have anything." Roy let out a sigh. "I didn't think I would need anything."

"You need more than a trick," Suki said. "He needs

to feel the way he makes you feel." Blob made Roy feel lots of ways: embarrassed, small, weak, scared, helpless. "He needs to be scared so bad that he will run from his own shadow and not know how to be mean anymore."

"I don't know," Roy said. "How would I ever scare him? And how would I know that would even work?"

"Nothing is ever for sure," Suki said, "But like in science, you have to test your hypothesis and wait for the results."

"I don't know about that."

"Well, you can't do nothing, that's for sure."

"I guess," Roy said. It was all he could say. He didn't know how to fix the Blob problem, but he had a feeling that Suki had some ideas.

Roy heard her footsteps come to a sliding stop in front of the house. He was beginning to understand why everyone thought it was haunted. The overgrown bushes and vines creeping up the sides created ominous shadows that looked like giant witches' hands casting a spell over a gurgling cauldron of sadness. He had passed by the house at least a thousand times, and it had never looked alive. But now, Roy swore he could see it breathing and licking its chops in anticipation of its next victim. The closed shutters and padlocked door appeared to be keeping something in—not out.

"Let's go around back," Roy heard Suki say. "C'mon."

He didn't follow her.

Instead, he watched the tall grass separate as Suki walked farther and farther away from him. It didn't take her long to create an uncomfortable gap between the two of them, so he sprinted up behind her. Roy was glad the invisible face shield hid his look of terror. Still, he tried to squash his fear and reason with Suki in a more practical tone. "Be careful. There could be snakes and stuff."

"Stop being so scared," Suki whispered back. "Spies aren't supposed to be scared."

"I'm not scared. But I'm not going to be stupid. Spies aren't stupid."

"You calling me stupid, Roy Winklesteen?" Suki stopped at a broken window near the patio.

"No . . . I know you're not stupid. But you do take a lot of risks."

"Yeah . . . and look how much fun I have." Roy could tell Suki was looking his way. "How much fun would you be having right now if you hadn't met me?"

"Okay, I get it." Roy tried looking in the window. "But this is just an old rundown house. It isn't fun . . . it's empty, so there's no one to spy on."

Suki didn't say anything as she pulled the flashlight from her pocket and aimed it at one of the windows. "You're right. It's just an empty house," she said. "I don't see any ghosts. It doesn't look scary—even at night."

"Yeah," Roy said, relieved she sounded disappointed and probably ready to head back.

"But . . . we could make it scary." Her voice had a frightful tone.

"Why would we want to do that?"

"Don't you see? This place is perfect."

"Perfect? For what?"

"To really teach Blob a lesson. To stop him from bothering you and plotting his revenge on Nicholas—for good."

"How's this place going to do that?"

"It's going to be the place where he gets the mean scared out of him—on Halloween night—all alone—with you and me and the invisibility spray."

CHAPTER 23

ENOUGH ALREADY.

Roy gave Suki an invisible grin. He liked her idea—sort of.

"Let's see if we can get inside and take a look around," Suki said, studying the back of the house with her flashlight.

They both walked around checking windows and doors. Everything was locked or stuck shut. This made Roy happy. He had no interest in going inside. First, he would be breaking the law. Second, he didn't want to not see any ghosts, and third, he didn't want any ghosts to not see him.

"I think we can scare Blob without going in," Roy whispered. "If we can get him into the backyard, we can use the spray to play all sorts of tricks on him—scary tricks."

Suki was still checking all the windows. She seemed determined to get in. "I guess. But imagine what we could do to him on the inside."

"Still, we can make it work. And besides, I need to get home. You know . . . school and all."

"Alright, let's go," Suki whispered, walking back toward the front of the house. "We need to get busy anyway. Halloween is the day after tomorrow."

Roy and Suki returned to the shed. They piled all the invisible gear back into the corner and sat down together at the mouse table. "How are we going to get Blob to the house?" Roy asked.

"Oh, that's easy." Suki looked especially confident. "You play him at his own game."

"Other than football...what's his game?"

"The tough-guy, I'm-not-afraid-of-anything game," she said. "We leave a note in his locker daring him to come to that house on Halloween night," she explained. "With the right words, Blob won't be able to resist the dare. Tough guys are all about proving that nothing scares them."

"But he doesn't even know you, and he won't care about me daring him."

"No . . . no." Suki looked exhausted from having to explain so much. "The note won't be from us—it won't be from anyone, really. Which makes it better because Blob won't risk looking weak in front of someone whose opinion he might care about."

Roy liked the idea of a plan to rid his life of Blob, but he wasn't convinced. "Okay, so we get him to the house, and we scare him. Then what?"

"Then he'll know what it's like to feel the way he makes other kids feel—terrified and helpless—then maybe he'll understand what he's doing. Remember, he has plans to scare Nicholas—or worse."

Roy tried to make sense of Suki's thinking. "I guess it might work."

"All we can do is try." She placed a pad of paper in front of the two of them. "Don't worry about it. We'll make sure there's no way for him to know it's you scaring him."

Roy agreed, and the two of them came up with the perfect note:

> YOU THINK YOU'RE SO TOUGH. PROVE IT.
> MEET ME AT THE BACK OF THE HAUNTED HOUSE IN YOUR NEIGHBORHOOD AT 7:30 ON HALLOWEEN NIGHT. IF YOU DON'T, THE ENTIRE SCHOOL WILL KNOW WHO THE WIMP REALLY IS.
> DON'T TELL ANYONE AND COME ALONE. I DARE YOU!

Suki folded up the note and tucked it under the pen.

"I'll put it in his locker tomorrow. Now, let's get started on how we can scare him."

They sketched and plotted for quite a while. When Roy checked the time, it was later than he thought. "Oh no, I need to get home." He glanced at the note. "Be careful tomorrow. Just because you're invisible doesn't mean someone can't detect you."

"Yeah . . . yeah. Whatever you say, Dad," Suki said, pushing him out the door. "Oh, thanks again for the cool gifts."

Roy stopped at the door. "No problem. I'll bring the stuff we need for our costumes."

"Okay, and I'll spray some old sheets so that we can go from visible to invisible really quick," Suki said. "I guess, when you think about it, we will be ghosts."

"All I care about is that we stop Blob from scaring me and wanting to kill Nicholas." Roy felt more determined than ever to get his life back. "But the sheets are a great idea."

As he crossed through Suki's front yard, Roy looked down the street at the abandoned house. He couldn't believe he had just been there—in the dark—around midnight. Was Suki inspiring him to be brave or only pressuring him to take risks that weren't worth the reward?

When he spent time with Bart, he had wanted to be brave because he wanted his life to be more exciting. Roy still wanted his life to be exciting and adventurous, but plotting revenge was not the same as flying off a roof. He felt like he was having to be brave for all the wrong reasons.

As he climbed the rope to his room, a long list of tricks filled his head. Imagining Blob screaming with fear did seem to make him feel better. For once, he would know what it was like to have all the power.

That morning on the bus was the worst yet. Nicholas rushed by Roy and met up with his friends in the back. Blob, again, made himself comfortable right next to Roy. "Your girlfriend still mad at ya, Tinkleweenie?" Blob said, staying put once Roy gave him his notebook. "Aw . . . I hate to see you two not getting along. I was looking forward to having to beat him up." He shrugged his broad shoulders. "That's okay. I'll get him anyway . . . it's not like you care what I do to him, right?"

Roy didn't say anything and looked straight ahead the entire ride. After hearing Blob's comment about

Nicholas, he no longer doubted that his and Suki's haunted house plan had to happen. He'd had enough of this guy. Halloween night couldn't arrive fast enough.

When the bus pulled up to the school, Roy exited as quickly as possible and didn't stop to find Suki or attempt to walk with Nicholas. For the rest of the school day, he avoided everyone by hanging out with the school nurse for fake stomach pains during P.E. and helping Ms. Crowley grade math tests at lunchtime. Roy felt smart and appreciated around her. She even shared her chips with him.

When he stepped onto the bus that afternoon, the girl behind the bus driver flagged him down. "You can sit here again," she said. She put her bookbag in her lap. "I don't mind."

Roy looked around at his other options and then scooched in next to her. He knew Suki was somewhere around and wished he could sit with her. "Thanks," he said.

"I'm Amelia," she said. "We have gym together."

"Oh . . . yeah . . . I think I've seen you around."

"I usually just watch. But once we start health, maybe we'll see each other more."

Roy nodded and tried to listen as Amelia continued to talk all the way to his bus stop.

That night in Suki's shed, the two friends nailed down their plans for frightening the nastiness out of Blob. Suki seemed to feel Roy's desperation, so she reassured him with information she had gotten at school.

"Everything is looking good," she said. "I saw Blob read the note, and I could tell he was thinking about it. He put it back in his locker without showing it to anyone."

"That's what we want, right?" Roy relaxed a little. "If he thought it was a joke or something, he would have shown it to his friends or thrown it away."

"Oh, he didn't act at all like it was a joke," Suki reassured him while ripping up an old shirt for her costume. "He'll show up because we dared him. He's too afraid of looking like a wimp if he doesn't make an appearance."

"Yeah . . . a guy like him would never ignore a dare." Roy let out a sigh of relief. "It's good to know he's afraid of something."

"He's afraid, alright. Why do you think he's so mean?" She leaned over Roy as he drew an outline of the house on a piece of paper. She nodded and then continued her analysis of Blob. "He's insecure and angry at something, so he wants other people to feel bad like him."

"Huh . . . he doesn't act insecure." Roy knew a lot about insecurity. In fact, he was a champion at it. If only it were an Olympic sport. Oh, the gold medals he would win.

"He's covering it up by being mean, and you're rewarding him for it by giving him power over you."

"I never thought about the fact that I was rewarding him."

"But you are. You do his homework for him," Suki said. "He could be nice and ask for your help, but he doesn't because he wants to look tough."

"Okay, so how is scaring him going to make him leave me alone?"

Suki looked up at the rough, wooden ceiling and thought for a minute. "Well . . . because right now, he's not scared or insecure enough. If he gets really scared, then he'll be afraid of everything . . . like you."

"What? I'm not sure I understand."

"Just trust me." She assembled a pile of supplies in the corner to take to the abandoned house. "If it doesn't do anything to him, at least it will do something for you."

"Like what?"

"REVENGE—ROY." Suki threw out her arms.

"Don't you want to scare him and feel like you have all the power? Isn't that why we are doing all of this? Maybe if you see him scared out of his mind, it will help you see that he's no different than anyone else. All humans get scared. Plus, don't you want to protect your best friend?"

Roy thought for a moment. Power... revenge—it all sounded so good to him. Maybe Suki was right. He had to do something. If not for himself, then for Nicholas, who had only been trying to help his wimpy friend.

Roy stopped thinking and got busy. His and Suki's plans included another visit to the abandoned house and lots of spray. He could hardly wait until tomorrow night.

CHAPTER 24

BOO!

Roy awoke with a big grin on his face. Although he knew the day would be miserable, he was confident the night would more than make up for it.

Suki caught up with him at his locker right before sixth period. He heard a whisper in his ear. "I saw Blob stick the note in his pocket. See you at the house."

The news put a big smile on Roy's face, and he actually talked to Amelia the whole way home. He didn't look back at all to see what Nicholas or Blob was doing. At that moment, he didn't care. He knew Suki would hear anything important and share it with him in a few hours.

Fortunately, Melonie had a costume emergency, and Roy spent the afternoon with his mom and sister at the Halloween store. He was able to get some rubber worms and fake blood to make his and Suki's costumes even scarier.

After an early dinner, all the Winklesteens prepared for the big night ahead. While his parents fussed over last-minute decorations and Melonie's costume, Roy got ready in his room. He finished up the final touches in the bathroom mirror and squinted at his reflection. The ripped and stained clothes, dark eye makeup, and rotting flesh tattoos made him look like he had been dead for at least a few weeks.

He filled his pack with supplies and told his parents he was meeting a group of friends at the bus stop. He included Suki in the list of kids all going trick-or-treating together, which made his parents very happy.

As he stepped outside, clusters of enthusiastic conversation and spurts of laughter filled the crisp fall air. Even though Halloween was his favorite night of the year, a hint of sadness bubbled up inside him. This was the first Halloween he wasn't spending with Nicholas. In the past, they had made the perfect trick-or-treating team. Nicholas liked anything chocolate, and Roy liked everything but chocolate, so trading was easy because neither of them got stuck with much candy they didn't like.

Roy wondered who his best friend was hanging out

with tonight. What costume did he decide on? Did he miss their friendship? Regardless, it was enough to know that Nicholas would have fun thanks to his and Suki's plans to distract Blob with their own prank.

By the time Roy reached the abandoned house, it was officially nighttime. His entire body felt tingly. As he looked around to make sure no one was watching him, he heard a faint voice.

"Roy, over here," Suki whispered from behind the overgrown shrubs on the side of the house. She wiggled the bush so Roy could track her down in the dark.

Roy looked around for any onlookers and then dashed over behind the bush.

"My parents are so happy I'm trick-or-treating with you." Suki giggled. "They think you are such a polite boy."

"Same here," Roy said. "My parents have been trying to make you my friend ever since they knew you might exist."

Suki gestured toward the back of the house. "I found an easy way in."

She walked to the sliding glass door. "You're not going to believe this." She pulled hard on the handle until it moved about one foot. "It was never locked. It was just stuck." She yanked Roy's tattered sleeve.

"C'mon."

"Wait." Roy leaned away from her. "I don't think we should. Our plans are all for outside."

"Don't be such a baby," Suki said, squeezing through the opening. "Things will work out better if we can use the inside." Suki took her flashlight from her bag and perused the room. "See? There's nothing to worry about, and we're not going to damage anything—not that it looks like it would matter."

Roy let out a faint whimper and followed Suki inside. "I don't think we should change anything. It's too risky."

"You already decided on the risk, Roy." Suki aimed the flashlight at his face. "Don't chicken out on me now. You want to get this guy back, don't you?"

"Well . . . yeah," Roy said. "That's why I don't want to change anything."

"We have time, and I've got some ideas." Suki sat down on the worn carpet and laid out everything from her bag.

Roy sat down next to her. They put their invisible gear on and updated their plans.

"See?" Suki said. "It will work even better now."

Roy looked at his watch. "We have about twenty minutes before Blob is supposed to show up." He picked up the flashlight between them and panned the light around the room.

"*Boooooooo*," whispered Suki, making a scary face. "Wanna look for ghosts?"

Roy looked around. The place was creepy and cold. He could barely see the staircase lurking in the front entry hall like it was daring him to venture into the unknown. Paper mixed with crunchy leaves littered the floor, and there was some graffiti on the wall. He felt better knowing he wasn't the only one who had broken the law. "I think we should stay put and wait for Blob."

"I knew I shouldn't have bothered asking." Suki took the flashlight and stood up. She was already halfway down a dark hall by the time Roy realized he was in the living room by himself. "I wonder why they didn't take all the furniture." Her voice was too faint for comfort. "That looks like a table we have in our house."

"Beats me," Roy whispered, rushing to catch up to her. "Maybe they didn't have room in their new place."

Suki wrapped both her hands around Roy's arm and pulled him close to her. "Or maybe they were murdered and don't need the furniture anymore," she said in a haunting voice.

Cruuunch . . . pop . . . squrush.

"Did you hear that?" Roy kept close to Suki.

Shroompt . . . thump.

"I heard that," Suki whispered.

Shrump . . . shrump . . . shrump.

"It's coming from out there—where all our stuff is." Suki turned around and crept back down the hall.

"Hey, whoever you are, I got the note. You'd better be here."

Roy reached out to stop Suki. "It's Blob. He's early."

"This way." Suki pulled Roy into a room off the hall.

"I guess I'm not the wimp—you are." Blob's voice cracked a little.

"He can't even tell time right. The note said seven-thirty," Roy whispered, pushing the invisible sheet back to reveal his watch. "What are we going to do? Our stuff is out there, and we are not in position."

"I'll stay inside and do what I can, and you sneak outside and go with what we had planned." Suki pushed Roy out the door and into the hall. "Remember, the sheet is invisible, so he can't see you," she whispered.

Roy sprinted down the hall.

"Hey? Is that you?" Blob called out from the kitchen. "So, what do you want?"

Roy ran past the kitchen door and scooped up what

he needed in the living room and slithered through the sliding door. He got into position and waited for Suki to make the first move.

"*Mmmmrrrrraaaahhhhh . . . auuuuuggggggghhh,*" Suki yelled out. "My arm . . . where's my arm?" Roy could barely see her limping into the living room.

"Who's there?" Blob peeped out of the kitchen doorway. "I'm gonna leave if you don't answer me."

Suki turned on the flashlight tucked inside her shirt. The beam of light lit up just the right parts of her decaying face and upper body. She began hobbling toward Blob. "My arm? Have you seen my arm?" she said, her voice quivering.

Roy shivered a little as he watched his friend. She was terrifying, alright. Her clothes were dirty and ragged with exposed patches of rotting flesh that oozed out wriggling worms clinging onto loose pieces of skin. Her left arm was wrapped in a sprayed towel, and the ketchup and fake blood concoction Roy had dripped onto her shoulder made it look like a bloody stump.

"My arm . . . did you eat my arm?" Suki said to Blob, staggering closer to him.

Blob screamed like a baby pig. "GET AWAY FROM ME." He ran out of the kitchen and dodged Suki as he stumbled into the living room. He tripped on Roy's bag of supplies and fell flat on his stomach just short of the sliding door.

Right as Blob got back on his feet, Roy got into position and took off his sunglasses. The only thing visible was his eyes—floating outside the door with a red beam of light shining into them.

"*MMMAAAAAAHHHH.*" Blob screamed again and turned away from the door toward the hall. Roy removed the invisible sheet and gloves and put on invisible sunglasses. As he entered the house, he held the flashlight above his head and followed the desperate screams. Blob was flailing and twirling about as an invisible Suki lunged at him with a bloody, floating arm. "Have you seen my body? My body—where's my body?"

Blob took off down the hall. Suki, the floating arm, and Roy followed him.

"My body?" Suki's voice quivered. "Where did you put my body?"

Roy did the same in his creepiest voice. "You took my eyes. I'm going to have to take your eyes."

Blob backed up into a room off the hall and covered his face. Suki and Roy kept coming closer, continuing to moan and talk in their scariest zombie voices.

Roy noticed a big wet spot growing on the front of

Blob's pants. He aimed the flashlight right at the spot. He looked over in Suki's direction and then saw the arm fly through the air and land at Blob's feet.

Blob curled up like a baby and slid down onto his bottom in the corner of the room. "MOMMYYYYY."

Roy felt Suki tug on his sheet, and the two of them slowly backed out of the room. They continued the spine-chilling talking and shuffling about until they saw Blob race into the living room and barely squeeze through the sliding door, sobbing the entire time.

In just seconds, the only sounds Roy could make out were grown-up voices and an occasional high-pitched "trick-or-treat." Suki removed all her invisible gear, and Roy took off his glasses. They both looked at each other and laughed—sort of.

"Man . . . was he scared," Suki said. "I guess we showed him."

Roy wasn't sure what to think, and he could tell Suki felt the same way.

"Do you think—maybe—we scared him too much?" Roy asked as they packed up all the supplies into an invisible bag.

"Does it matter? What about all the times he scared you and tried to beat up Nicholas?" Suki headed out the sliding door. "He should have never been mean to you."

For a few moments, Roy battled with his guilty thoughts before allowing himself to enjoy their success. "You're right. He did get what he deserved."

"He should leave you and Nicholas alone now—that's for sure," she said. "No one can be that scared and not change from it."

They both looked around to see if anyone was watching and then ran onto the sidewalk. "You're right. He's bound to change from such a horrifying experience," Roy said with questionable relief. Change—that's what he wanted to see in Blob. He couldn't get much meaner, so any change would have to be for the better.

Hopefully, Roy thought. He was going to get his life back—boring days and all.

The two of them joined some other trick-or-treaters for a last-minute candy haul. Suki's house was their last stop. "You did good tonight, Roy Winklesteen," she said, patting him on the shoulder.

Roy reached into his candy bag. "You too. Thanks for your help. I guess I should be glad you're a know-it-all."

Suki shoved a candy bar into her mouth. "So, is revenge as sweet as that Twizzler you're snarfing down?"

Roy smiled. "Are you kidding me? Revenge is much sweeter, and it should last a lot longer."

"Definitely," Suki said. "By the way, coloring the flashlight lens red made you look extra scary. That was a good idea."

"Thanks, it was the easiest thing we did." Roy let out a big laugh. "I can't believe he wet his pants. He's got some nerve calling me Tinkleweenie."

Suki was laughing so hard that she choked a little on her candy bar. "Yeah, maybe you should bring the arm. Then he'll realize what a big chicken he was when he sees it was nothing but a ripped shirt sleeve stuffed with socks and a glove on the end—oh, and fake blood mixed with ketchup."

"Nah . . . that might un-scare him," Roy said. "I want him to believe the house is really haunted. I want him to be scared every time he passes by the place."

"Think he'll tell anyone?" Suki asked.

"If he does, he won't tell the truth."

Suki nodded. "It doesn't matter. He knows the truth, and so do we."

"Yeah, that's the good thing about truth. It's always there, no matter how much everyone ignores it."

Suki pulled the arm stump from her bag and aimed the gloved end at Roy. "Friends?"

Roy shook the glove. "Friends," Roy said, turning back toward his house. "See ya."

"No, you won't see me. But I'll be there," Suki said. "I wouldn't miss tomorrow for anything."

Roy was so happy, he felt like he was floating. He never thought it would feel so good to make someone else feel so bad. For once, he had all the power. He almost understood why Blob acted the way he did.

CHAPTER 25

OUCH!

Melonie greeted Roy at the front door. "How much did you get?" she asked, trying to take a peek inside Roy's bag.

"Enough," he said, yanking his bag away from her.

"Roy, is that you?" his mom said from the stairs. "Did you have fun?"

"Yeah . . . it was the best Halloween ever."

"Is that so?" his dad asked, walking up behind his mom. "What made this particular Halloween so great?"

Roy smirked. "Just had fun scaring people, that's all."

"Well, I hope you didn't scare any little kids." His mom's voice was not as cheery.

"No . . . actually . . . teenagers. One guy screamed like a baby pig,"

His dad snickered. "Nothing wrong with that. That's who you should be scaring. I was too afraid to go near teenagers when I was your age."

His mom looked at his dad with a disagreeable look. "Well, I'm glad everyone had a good time, but I'm glad the night is over. I've had enough of zombies and princesses. It's time for a bath—then it's off to sleep. C'mon Melonie."

Roy stashed all the invisible gear in his closet until he could bring it to Suki's the next night. He took the longest shower of his life and had to scrub extra hard to get off all the makeup, tattoos, and fake blood. While he changed into his pajamas, Roy stole a quick peek out his window. It was almost impossible to believe that earlier that night, he had made the biggest, scariest guy at school wet his pants.

As he collapsed into bed, he replayed the prank over and over again in his mind. He stuffed the covers in his mouth to muffle his laughs. He couldn't sleep, and he was pretty sure Blob couldn't sleep either—but for an entirely different reason.

Revenge—what an awesome feeling, he thought. The night had worked out better than he and Suki had planned.

Friday morning started out like any other morning. Nicholas walked by Roy and sat in the back of the bus with his friends. He looked happy—which meant Blob hadn't ruined his night—and that made Roy happy. The two gave each other a quick glance, but that was it. Roy wanted to tell Nicholas all about Halloween night and all the other nights. But he couldn't—ever.

Instead, he sat alone—waiting.

As the bus squealed up to the worst stop on the route, Roy began to sweat a little. This was it. If everything went as planned, Blob would walk right past him, sit with the other eighth-graders, and never waste his time on lowly sixth-graders again. That's what any normal teenager would do. Right?

But was it possible to scare the meanness out of someone? Had the haunted house prank really changed Blob?

Plomp . . . plomp . . . plomp.

There it stood.

Its shadow darkened the first few rows of seats.

It looked as huge and mean as ever.

It swaggered down the aisle, causing a wave of silence as it proceeded deeper into the bus.

Roy knew better than to look right at it, but he couldn't resist.

Then it happened—just like all the other mornings. Its eyes shifted in Roy's direction and locked in on him like an eagle honing in on its prey. It let out a satisfied chuckle as it noticed the empty space where Nicholas used to sit.

That's when Roy knew. It hadn't changed. It was still the same Blob it had always been.

Roy had no choice but to face the truth. Blob may have been scared of kid zombies and floating arms, but he wasn't the least bit scared of Roy. Why would he be? He had been invisible.

As far as Blob was concerned, Roy was the same powerless kid today that he had been yesterday.

Still, something seemed different.

Roy no longer felt powerless.

Suki was right. Blob was only human, and all humans can be and feel vulnerable. Halloween night had proven that. Roy finally realized that the easiest way to gain power over someone was to feed off of their weaknesses. For Roy, his insecurity and kindness made him an obvious target for Blob, and Blob's predictability and ego had made him susceptible to his and Suki's pranks.

It all made sense to Roy. No wonder Blob didn't want to change. Power was more tempting to guzzle down than an open bag of Doritos with no one around to have to share it with.

Roy started to feel a little queasy. What had he done? Even worse, who had he become?

As he watched Blob *plomp* closer to his seat, Roy might as well have been looking in the mirror. The invisibility spray had done precisely what Suki's grandmother had feared. It had transformed two good kids into vengeful, cruel, and unaccountable beasts that only had one goal in mind—to make someone feel bad. And what was worse, they had gotten away with it.

Roy's breathing picked up. He wrung his hands. Was he evil? Had that swig of potion from the invisibility gods turned him into the very person he despised the most? Was he doomed to walk among the haters for the rest of his life?

Roy shifted his gaze out the window. He could no longer look at Blob, and he knew he would not be able to face his reflection in the mirror until he tried to make everything right. Roy could no longer hide behind Nicholas, the bus driver, Suki, invisibility spray, fear, excuses, or pranks.

It was time for Roy to take action—the kind

everyone could see.

"Move over, Tinkleweenie." Blob began to aim his backside toward the seat.

Roy felt his all-too-familiar sponge of insecurity attempt to absorb every bit of confidence he tried to release. But this time, the soft and weak parasite was no match for Roy's determination. He squeezed it dry until it disintegrated into a pile of dust in the pit of his stomach.

Roy looked his worst nightmare right in the eyes. "You're not going to copy my homework. But I'll help you with it."

"Help?" Blob looked as though Roy was talking to him in some bizarre foreign language. "I don't need your help, you little stain. I could do algebra if I wanted, but I don't want to."

Roy lifted his backpack and placed it in the empty part of the seat next to the window. He then made himself bigger by spreading his legs wider and putting his hand flat on his pack.

"Then there's no room," Roy said in his deepest voice.

Blob curled his upper lip. "Move it, moron. I'm not going to tell you again." His behind continued to make its way right toward Roy's face.

Roy bent his arm and jabbed his elbow into Blob's hip. "I said, there's no room."

Blob stepped back into the aisle right as the bus squealed up to the last stop. He turned around and gave Roy an extra-long death stare. Kids from the stop started piling up behind Blob's massive body like soapy water struggling to get past a clump of tangled hair in a bathtub drain.

The door closed, but the bus didn't move. No one did, and the only sound was the low hum of the idled engine.

Blob looked at the bus driver. The bus driver looked at him. "Fine. Whatever . . . you little loser." He took the empty seat across from Roy.

The bus shifted into gear and took off down the road. The air filled with cautious chatter. Roy looked at Blob. Blob scowled back at Roy.

He extended his arm. "Give it here, Tinkleweenie. Don't be stupid. It's not your style."

Roy ignored him and focused his eyes toward the front of the bus.

Blob stretched his thick leg across the aisle and thumped the side of Roy's knee with his shoe. "You heard me." Blob checked the bus driver's eyes in the rearview mirror. "Don't make me hurt you. Remember, your little girlfriend isn't here to protect you."

Roy looked back at Nicholas. His former best friend was staring right at him. "You need to do your own homework," Roy said in his loudest voice. "It's the only way you're going to learn anything."

Blob stood up and leaned over Roy. "What makes you think I wanna learn anything—especially math? I'm not gonna need algebra to be a pro football player."

Blob was so close to Roy's face that he could see up his nose—and it wasn't pretty—but Roy felt like Blob might actually be listening to him. "Math's a good thing to know for football because the game is all about strategy and timing. A lot of football players are really smart."

"You saying I'm not smart?" Blob slapped Roy's pack on the floor and planted his knees on the seat. He gripped Roy's t-shirt right below his chin and raised his fist—which seemed to be his response to anything he didn't like hearing.

Roy looked up at the fist. It looked as big as his face. Should he close his eyes? Was it going to hurt? Would he lose any teeth? How bad was he going to bleed? What would his parents say?

Roy closed his eyes, tightened his jaw, and prepared for a massive dose of pain.

"HEY. Leave him alone." Roy opened his eyes. There was Nicholas, standing right next to the icky seat, staring Blob down. "Why don't you pick on someone your own size. He's only trying to help you. Why are you so mean?"

Blob turned toward Nicholas, his fist still clenched and ready for release. He let go of Roy and pushed Nicholas onto the icky seat. He drew his fist back even further and then thrust it right at Nicholas's face.

But his fist didn't hit Nicholas.

Instead, it slammed into Roy's backpack, which happened to contain a very heavy algebra book, now perfectly positioned in front of Nicholas's face.

Blob jerked his hand back and stood up in the aisle. "Ouch." While shaking his wrist, he sucked in a hissing breath through his teeth.

Nicholas lifted up both feet, planted them on Blob's stomach, and straightened out his legs. Blob fell back onto the kids sitting across the aisle. They screamed and pushed him away.

Screeeeeeeeeeeeeeeeechhhhh.

The bus stopped on the side of the road. The driver got up and rushed to the commotion. He pulled Blob up by his shoulders. "I told you I didn't want any of this on my bus."

Nicholas realized what seat he was lying on and climbed over next to Roy. The bus driver forced Blob down onto the icky seat. "Don't move. Don't talk. And don't get off this bus until I say so." The bus driver returned to his seat and continued on to school.

Roy and Nicholas looked at each other. Then they looked at Blob.

"You're right," Roy said. "I should've never given him my homework the first time."

"That's okay." Nicholas looked at Roy like he used to, before middle school. "It's not your fault that you're smart."

Even over all the enthusiastic conversation, Roy could hear Blob huffing and growling. But he wasn't worried. He had his confidence and his best friend back, and together they could conquer anything Blob hurled their way.

No doubt, Roy had learned his lesson. Like a poisoned apple, revenge hid its bite of bitterness behind a tempting disguise of sweet satisfaction. Just a nibble had almost choked Roy beyond recognition. But the old Roy had fought to stay alive and found his way back to his best friend—and it felt amazing.

The bus finally pulled up to the front of the school. When Roy and Nicholas stepped onto the school sidewalk, a small crowd of kids gathered around them.

"Whoa . . . I can't believe you stood up to that guy," one of Nicholas's new friends said.

"If he bothers you again, we'll back you up," another kid said among a group of eighth-graders.

"You're so brave," Amelia said, giving Roy a dreamy look. "I'm so glad he didn't hurt your face. You have a nice smile."

Nicholas snickered and gave Roy a gentle push of admiration. "Alright . . . Winklesteen."

The crowd turned toward the bus, where they could see Blob getting chewed out by the driver. Roy felt a 2000-pound weight of worry tumble off his shoulders as he heard the man telling Blob he would have to find another way to and from school.

Everyone watched Blob *plomp* onto the sidewalk. "What are you looking—"

"We're not looking at anything," one of the eighth-graders said, moving in front of Roy and Nicholas. "And there's nothing here for you. I think you should just go to class." A couple of other guys stepped forward and stood next to him. Together, they created a force even Blob knew better than to mess with.

Roy's former nightmare let out one last huff as he walked away from the crowd. He looked back at Rob.

"Well . . . c'mon. We don't need these losers."

Rob didn't move, and his face made it clear to Blob that he had no intention of following. Instead, he stayed behind with all the other kids until the school bell summoned everyone to their first-period class. Nicholas and Roy lagged behind. They wanted to take a few seconds to soak in the moment together.

"Thanks for blocking that punch," Nicholas said, nudging Roy. "My face especially thanks you."

Roy laughed and nudged him back. "No problem. Thanks for distracting him with your face."

Nicholas looked away for a few seconds. "Sorry, I didn't stick by you. I've been a jerk."

"No . . . you did what you had to do." Roy looked his friend right in the eyes. "You were right all along. I should've stuck up for myself. You tried to help me, but I still gave in to him. It was all my fault. So, I needed to fix it—without magic—without anything but me."

"Still . . . I shouldn't have ignored you like that. I won't ever do it again. I promise."

"Me too." Roy glanced toward the eighth-grade wing. "I hope he's learned his lesson."

"Don't worry about it. He's not your problem anymore. Me and all the other guys will make sure of that."

"I think he will probably still be a problem." Roy felt an earthquake of confidence rumble through his body. "But I'm pretty sure I can handle it."

The two friends entered their louder-than-usual English class. Nicholas gave Roy a joking shove. "Looks like we've made the Gossip Gazette again. I wonder how much the story has changed."

"I won't say anything if you won't," Roy said.

"Deal," Nicholas said.

CHAPTER 26

BRAVO.

The only thing that could have made the school day better was if it had happened at night. Roy had gotten back all the things in his life he had allowed Blob to steal from him: his best friend, his pride, and his love of math, to name a few. Even better, he had learned a great deal about what it's like to be bullied and what it's like to be a bully.

Both were terrible.

Meanness was like the flu—it's miserable when it's happening to you and very easy to spread around. He knew he hadn't completely rid his life of Blob or any other future blobs. Nevertheless, he felt wise enough to know what to do if the dreaded situation occurred again.

So far, everything looked promising. Blob didn't say

anything in math class, and the ride home confirmed that he was banned from public school transportation for the rest of the year. Roy waited around at the bus stop and called out to Suki, but she didn't respond.

That night, as Roy entered her lab, she greeted him with a shower of confetti. "Way to go, Winklesteen." She threw a fist full of colorful paper squares Roy's way. "YOU DID IT."

Roy brushed some confetti off his shoulders. "Thanks, I guess it was a pretty good day."

"Just good?" Suki plucked a couple of pieces out of his hair. "Not great?"

They both sat down at the mouse table. An awkward silence filled the compact space. There was a lot to say, and Roy could tell neither of them knew how to say it. But Roy had to get some things to get off his chest, so he got the ball rolling.

"Okay... it was a great day." He sensed Suki's concern, so he smiled really big. "I guess I never needed the invisibility spray to begin with. You and Nicholas were right. I should've stood up to him the first day he wanted my homework—especially since Nicholas was willing to back me up. I should've never been such a wimp."

"You're not a wimp." Suki had an expression on her

face that Roy had never seen before. "There's something I need to tell you—something I found out about Blob."

Suki's tone scared Roy a little. "What? It's nothing—"

"No . . . it's nothing for you to worry about. As a matter of fact, it's good news."

"Well . . . then why are you acting like you shouldn't tell me?"

"Because I found out about it the day before Halloween."

"Why didn't you tell me then?"

"Because I didn't want you to back out of our haunted house plans."

"Why would I back out?"

"Because Blob's last day at your school was today."

For the moment, all Roy could feel was relief. "Blob's last day at the school"—a phrase Roy had dreamed of hearing for quite a while. He was afraid to blink for fear of opening his eyes and discovering the moment was just a dream. If this was another one of Suki's jokes, he was most certainly done with her. "Did he get expelled for what he did on the bus?"

"No, he's not expelled." Suki looked down at her fidgeting hands. "He's transferring to another school—

a strict school—for kids like him—with anger problems and other stuff."

"How do you know all of this?" Roy asked. "Did you spy on him talking to Rob?"

"No. I sat in on a meeting the principal had with Blob and his parents. It's a sleep-away school. So, you really won't have to deal with him."

"Sleep-away? Like some sort of military school or something?" Roy had nightmares about places like that. Sure, they weren't all bad. But he doubted Blob was going to one where the kids wanted to be there.

"I'm not sure if it's a military school, but Blob looked scared. Apparently, the plans for him to transfer there have been in place since the beginning of October."

"So, the haunted house prank was a waste of time?" Roy felt even worse about what he and Suki had done to Blob. He picked up Uno and began stroking her on the head. Her warm softness was a comforting distraction from what was turning out to be quite an eye-opening conversation. "If he knew he was leaving, then why did he ever bother me for my homework? What was the point?"

"Like I said before, it was never about your homework. It was about Blob making you feel bad so he felt better."

"It all seems so stupid."

"If you'd seen Blob with his dad, it would make more sense to you."

"His dad? Why would he have anything to do with Blob and me?"

"Because his dad is meaner than Blob and gets angry at him," she said. "He even called Blob a disappointment—in front of the principal."

"So, Blob was mean to me because his dad was mean to him. And we were mean to Blob because he was mean to Nicholas and me."

"Exactly."

"What a mess." Roy returned Uno to the bin. "Why do humans make everything so complicated?"

"I don't know. Maybe it's because our brains tell us to do one thing, but our feelings want to do something else, so it all turns into one giant mess. I'm sorry I didn't tell you about Blob Wednesday night. I just wanted you to have some power over him so you could see that he was no different than the rest of us. I thought I was helping you, but the pranks didn't help. You didn't need my help. You turned out to be braver than I ever could have been."

"That's okay. You were trying to do something good

for me." Suki looked the way Roy felt when he realized he had fallen victim to the very thing Suki's grandmother had feared. "I understand why you did what you did—why I did what I did—and why Blob did what he did. None of us were right, but at least you and I figured that out. I guess all we can hope is that Blob does too."

"He looked so pathetic sitting next to his dad," Suki murmured, seeming to hide her face behind her long, black hair. "I guess I feel kind of sorry for him. And I'm sorry for pressuring you to do all that stuff to him. It's just that you're so nice, and I hated seeing you so sad. Everything seemed like such a good idea at the time."

"You have some of the best ideas . . . ever," Roy said. "We just used them the wrong way. Even so, thanks for trying to help me. You're a nice person too."

Suki hooked her hair behind her ears. She looked relieved. "Middle school is the worst. I'm not sure I would want to go if I couldn't be invisible."

"But I'd like it if you were visible. It's hard knowing you're there, wondering what you are doing, and not really being able to talk to you."

"You don't have to worry about me being there anymore. I've had enough of your school for now."

Roy wasn't sure how to feel. At first, Suki's invisible

presence at school unnerved him, but he had gotten to where he liked knowing she was there. What kid wouldn't want an invisible friend looking out for them?

"What? You're not going to go anymore?"

"No, it's hard being invisible. I had to stay out of everyone's way, and I couldn't talk. Do you have any idea how hard it was for me to keep my opinion to myself?"

"Yes, I know exactly how hard it was for you." He laughed.

Suki laughed back. "Jeez, some of those kids have no idea what they are talking about, and everyone listens to them anyway."

"You're right about that," Roy said. "Still, I'd like it if you were there."

"Thanks . . . but I have my own school work to do. And I still have to figure out a formula that won't make me invisible."

"But you're going to keep the old formula, aren't you?" Roy tried not to sound too worried. "I think we learned our lesson. Your grandmother was right. The spray should be kept a secret."

Suki glanced over at the locked cabinet. "I wonder if my grandmother is disappointed in me."

"I don't think so. Sure . . . we took things too far,"

Roy reasoned. "But now we really understand what your grandmother feared. And that means we will respect the power of the spray even more."

Suki fell back into her chair. She looked tired. "I guess I will keep the spray locked up for now."

Roy didn't feel the need for Suki to take such extreme measures. After all, it was invisibility spray. He wasn't about to let something like that stay locked up in a banged-up old cabinet. "Don't feel bad. We're bound to figure out something good to use the spray for. Isn't that what a scientist would do—keep trying?"

Suki's face brightened. "And I guess until we can do good with it, there's nothing wrong with having a little fun—at no one else's expense, of course."

"Exactly." Roy was glad to see the adventurous side of Suki return. He didn't like seeing her worried. That was his job. "So, what can I do to help you get the spray to work the way your grandmother wanted?"

"I was hoping you would say that," Suki said. "I was afraid you were only my friend because of the whole invisibility thing."

"Nah," Roy said. "Well . . . maybe a little in the beginning. But that's because you kept teasing me with all those big secrets and making me feel dumb. I wasn't sure what to think of you."

"Yeah . . . I guess I can be a lousy friend sometimes."

"I think everyone can be a lousy friend sometimes," Roy reassured her. "But real friends understand that."

He could tell Suki wasn't sure what to say. So, she kept it short and sweet. "I guess you're right."

Roy, on the other hand, knew exactly what to say. "I think Nicholas should meet you. We would all make such a great team."

"I was hoping you would say that too," she said. "In case you hadn't noticed, I don't have a lot of friends. Moving all the time and having to stay indoors has always made it hard to meet other kids."

"Well . . . you've got a friend now, and I'm sure Nicholas will like you. I just need to convince him that being a nightlifer is much more exciting than anything daylifers have to offer."

Suki smirked. "I'm sure, with enough proof, it won't be too hard to convince him."

The two friends joked and laughed until their bellies hurt. They tried to get started on a new formula, but conversations about past events kept distracting them. Neither one seemed to mind, though.

Roy returned to his room much later than any other night. He tucked himself deep into his covers and let his brain wind down with a few last thoughts.

So far, middle school had been quite an adventure. He had Suki to thank for that. Perhaps some situations had gone too far, but he'd done his best to make things right.

Without a doubt, being invisible—on purpose—was as awesome as flying like a bird. But being invisible because you weren't doing anything worthy of being seen was the worst—and Roy vowed to never feel that way again.

For the first time in over two weeks, he drifted off to sleep with nothing but good thoughts gently luring him deep into dreamland.

Click ... click ... clank.

Roy's eyes sprung open.

He sat up and looked toward the noise.

Click ... click.

Something was hitting his window.

Was it Suki? Roy wondered.

He jumped out of bed and opened the sash.

He looked down at the ground under the big oak tree.

It wasn't Suki.

He blinked several times. He couldn't believe his eyes.

"Bart? Is that you?"

**Be sure to read
the first adventure.**

**There are more adventures to come!
www.sallydill.com**

ABOUT THE AUTHOR

Sally Dill is a proud nightlifer who doesn't think that anyone should have to apologize for being productive while most are sleeping and sleeping a little while most are productive. If it weren't for the quiet solitude of the night, she probably would have never become an author.